T0194693

# WANNA SUCCEED?

## CUSTOMER SERVITUDE

### Your Servant

WESTBOW
PRESS®
A DIVISION OF THOMAS NELSON
& ZONDERVAN

WestBow Press books may be ordered through booksellers or by contacting:

WestBow Press
A Division of Thomas Nelson & Zondervan
1663 Liberty Drive
Bloomington, IN 47403
www.westbowpress.com
844-714-3454

Scripture taken from the King James Version of the Bible.

ISBN: 978-1-6642-2117-8 (sc)
ISBN: 978-1-6642-2118-5 (hc)
ISBN: 978-1-6642-2150-5 (e)

Library of Congress Control Number: 2021901718

Print information available on the last page.

WestBow Press rev. date: 2/2/2021

# OUR JOURNEY TOGETHER

Hi, I'm your servant. I'm the one who wants to see you achieve true success. I'm the one who wants everyone to achieve true success. Know anyone who doesn't want to achieve success? You and I are gonna go even further, and focus on TRUE Success. It took me many years to figure out how to define and achieve true success, and I still never did it on my own. By journaling my journey, I want to make a more comfortable ride for you on your personal journey. As my dad would often say, "Nobody ever said it was gonna be easy." Sometimes challenges placed in our path seem so impossible, we think it would be easier to get a camel through the eye of a needle. This is why as your servant, I'm offering myself to assist you in any way I can. Keep your hands and feet inside the ride at all times and hold on tight while we experience true success together. **Philippians 4:13: "I can do all things through Christ which strengtheneth me."**

## • • • •
# EVERYTHING IS SALES

Yes, everything is sales.

If you never sell your parents, siblings, relatives, friends, on who you are, they'll never trust or believe in you. If you can't sell your employer on who you are, they'll never hire you, or keep you employed. If you don't sell your spouse on who you are, they won't stay with you. When we're out in the trenches doing our part in the great commission, if we aren't for real, how can we sell anyone on the only opportunity there is for everlasting life? Everything is sales. **Proverbs 11:30: "The fruit of the righteous is a tree of life, and he that winneth souls is wise."**

I would have given anything if someone had told me very early on in life that everything is sales. More importantly, I wish someone had told me what it really took to truly succeed in this world. If I properly sell my heart's desire to you, you'll read all that I have to share, and, hopefully, I can serve many people in many positive ways. **Proverbs 16:3:**

**"Commit thy works unto the Lord, and thy thoughts shall be established."**

I've asked others for years who the greatest salesperson of all time is. When referring to those who are "of this world," my answer is Andy Griffith. In the 1960s, when he portrayed Sheriff Andy Taylor on "The Andy Griffith Show," he was the ultimate diplomat. He didn't carry a gun, didn't wear a fancy ornamented uniform, almost always had a hand in his pocket, and could solve any conflict with sensible reasoning and compassion. Sheriff Andy Taylor sincerely cared for others. In turn, everyone trusted and believed in him. It's an old saying, but very true, "People don't care how much you know, 'til they know how much you care."

Years later, Andy Griffith reemerges on TV as "Matlock," where he wears the same plain suit almost all of the time, almost always has a hand in his pocket, and almost always achieves his objective. "Man's" sales textbook says never put your hands in your pockets. To me, hands in pockets make one appear non-threatening, unassuming, and humble. For years, I approached many places of business with such humility, so I wouldn't give the impression of John Wayne bustin' through saloon doors. Thank you Lord; I never went hungry.

To put everything into proper perspective, the greatest salesperson of all time is the only one to take the nails for all, and the only one to ever defeat death. Someone laid their life down for me? I'm sold! This is who I work for, this is my boss, this is who owns me, this is my inspiration, this is my purpose for breath. With only one being through whom eternal life is achieved, what else is there? **John 14:6: "Jesus saith unto him, I am the way, the truth, and the life: no man cometh unto the Father, but by me."**

# • • • •
# HOW IT ALL
# STARTED

From the age of 12 to 30, my primary vocation was playing drums. My mom purchased my first drum set for $150, and it looked like something Ringo would've used in his early years with "The Beatles." As kids, my sister and I would always have to save up our money if we wanted something. I couldn't believe my mom was paying for this drum set. Next thing you know, I'm an indentured servant in my mom's gospel trio. Do you think I had any clue at the time that there was no greater privilege than to serve our Lord? I never received any money for playing with my mom's gospel group. We played two kinds of gigs: those with a pot luck meal afterwards, and those without.

In high school, I got to play rock and country music for money, and thought that was the greatest thing. Since I was never gonna get paid to play baseball professionally, playing drums for money seemed like the next best thing. I left home a few weeks after high school graduation and eventually migrated to Nashville, where I got to do things that those who are of this world think are kinda neat. Of course, kinda neat aspirations cannot compare to anything Eternal. Nowadays, when people find out all of the things I got to do from playing the drums, most want to ask "Who did you play for?" I always respond with "The best group I was ever a part of, was Wayne Shadden's Thursday night men's Bible study." After quitting drumming cold turkey for 13 years, I was shown by the only One who is in charge that it don't mean a thing, unless you're playin' for The King. Now I play for the Lord as many Sunday mornings as I can.

For the next 18 years, my primary vocation was officially in sales. What better career move, since musicians are basically unemployed every day when they wake up and constantly have to sell themselves? Everything is sales! With multiple regional and national sales honors and achievements in this temporary world, at the age of 48, I was ready for more. Recognition from man is a nice thing; recognition from God is everything.

# THANK YOU, LORD, FOR EXPRESS LUNCH

Since the most important thing in the universe is the One who created the universe, I desired a full-time vocation working for Him. I don't perceive myself as a pulpit guy, but I said, "Lord, if you'll provide me with a brick and mortar location, where I can make at least $25,000 a year income, I'll be  your head custodian at this facility." Next thing you know, I'm at Express Lunch, which was a nine-year-old operation at the time. At Express Lunch, there's a large cooler filled with salads, sandwiches, and wraps to go, and also seating for folks who want to dine in. Take one guess who cleans the commodes every morning? I'm the custodian alright, and there's no greater privilege. I'm also the last one to leave after "swabbin' the deck." Hey, if Carol Burnett wasn't too good to mop up before locking up, neither am I.

At first, I was a little nervous at Express Lunch, since I had never run a cash register in my life. My first prayer was, "Lord, may I never overcharge anybody, so they don't think I'm trying to rip them off." My subsequent prayer has been, "Lord, may everyone see you, when they see me." Years earlier, I had defined myself as a servant. I don't want to be any more than a servant; I don't want to be any less than a servant. My responsibility is to make sure that our Lord is properly represented to the best of my ability at Express Lunch. This requires me to be totally emptied of myself, which is never easy, and filled with whatever the Lord wants for Express Lunch. Our business model is "We surrender the place to the Lord, and He blesses us way beyond our imagination." Guess what? He has, like never before! There is no greater privilege in this world than to serve our Lord and Master. Every day, I get to love folks up one side and down the other. I cannot tell you how blessed I am, which is why I want to help anyone I can with all of the many things I've humbly learned so far over the past 6+ years serving at Express Lunch. Here's where it starts:

# WE HAVE TO BE THE EXCEPTION

Being exceptional doesn't mean being better than anyone; it means being non-typical. No human being is "better" than any other human being. God doesn't love any one person more than another; He doesn't love any one person less than another. In a world where everyone is homogeneously running around saying "no problem, no problem, no problem, no problem" all of the time, there's tremendous opportunity for an aspiring servant to display their uniquely created heart and soul by being the exception! **Exodus 19:5: "Now therefore, if ye will obey my voice indeed, and keep my covenant, then ye shall be a PECULIAR TREASURE unto me above all people: for all the earth is mine."**

Once we've identified The Greatest Salesperson of All Time, it becomes real easy to subsequently identify The Greatest Sales Manual of All Time: THE BIBLE. There are many references in the Bible as to how we are not to be "of this world." So to each reference, I just keep saying "yes Sir," "yes Sir," yes Sir," yes Sir," to the Almighty's instruction, and try my best to run as far and fast away from how "man" does things as I can! **John 17:16: "They are not of the world, even as I am not of the world."** Kinda like when an investment "professional" tells you that they know which direction the stock market is going to go. Run as far and as fast as you can in the other direction! No matter how many fancy college degrees we have, none of us know what direction the stock market is gonna go. **Psalm 119:10: "With my whole heart I have sought thee: O let me not wander from thy commandments."**

The question I get asked the most at Express Lunch is, "Are you the owner?" to which I get the privilege and OPPORTUNITY of saying "Oh no, The Lord owns this place; I'm nothin but a servant." What better way to be the exception, than with humility? What answer is every restaurant "owner" who is of this world gonna give? Picture Mr. Ziffel from "Green Acres" clutching his bibby overalls with his thumbs, and his head cocked back saying with the utmost pride, "I shore am, lock, stock, and barrel." The fact is, we'll never own anything in this world, other than our Savior. Everything is God's! Our children aren't even ours; they're His. I might be the dad, but I'm not the Father. We are HIS children, and eventually every knee shall bow, and every tongue shall confess to God. I sure hope we don't get "above our raising" and forget that come judgement day, everyone will be reminded that He owns all of our back sides. Once again, another example of how every day I can proclaim without shame the greatness of God, and how He's blessed us! What greater vocation than to be a servant?

The second most frequently asked question at Express Lunch is, "How do you remember everybody's name?" My immediate response is, "I don't." Or people will say, "I sure wish I had your memory," and I'll immediately say, "I wish I did too." One day, a customer rattled off all of man's memory techniques, none of which I had ever heard of. I'm kinda familiar with what they call "association." We have a couple that comes in, Fred and Betty. Well, that one's easy. We associate Fred and Betty with "The Flintstones" cartoon. The only problem is, in "The Flintstones" cartoon, Fred is married to Wilma, and Betty is married to Barney. We'll move on from there. The answer to "How do you remember everybody's name" is very fundamental: I owe it to all customers who come through the door to remember their names. As consumers, we have many big name franchised eating places to choose from. If someone cares enough to try out a little self-proprietor eating location, I have to care even more about them. Another OPPORTUNITY to extend gratitude. When we go into a big name franchise, do we know who the proprietor is? If I do my job correctly, everyone knows that the Lord owns

Express Lunch. If someone cares enough about helping me feed my family, I have to care even more about how well that customer's family is fed.

To me, it feels like I only remember every 2 out of 3 names. The name remembering bar isn't very high in this world, which makes for great OPPORTUNITY! Seems like we always remember a face, and we always forget a name. We're so blessed with so many people coming through the door of Express Lunch; I can't keep up with all of the names any more. Do you like it when someone cares about you? Do you like it when someone cares enough about you to remember your name? When I first quit playing drums for a living in Nashville, I started doing limo driving. We did all kinds of transportation: celebrity events, late night party runs, airport transfers, you name it. With the airport transfers, there was the opportunity to meet many more various degrees of people. When I would meet customers, I would immediately introduce myself as their chauffeur. The very few times anyone ever remembered my name, I would just about be in shock. What a great opportunity to see how many people care, or don't care, about you.

One late night, I drove James Stroud and his wife home from the airport. I had seen James Stroud play drums on quite a few occasions. He was a hard-hitting drummer who played with total confidence, command, and authority. I loved his playing. At this time, Mr. Stroud had worked his way up to being a very successful recording industry executive, and it was an honor to serve him. All the way to his residence, Mr. Stroud called me by my name. James Stroud treated me with respect, and of course, I have the utmost respect for him. Funny thing, James Stroud is an exception, a success, and the person who taught me the importance of learning names. May James Stroud be a True Success to the only One that matters. To me, remembering names falls under the category of what we mentioned earlier: "People don't care how much you know, 'til they know how much you care."

I forgot about this one, until my wife and I drove through Chattanooga recently. A friend and his girlfriend were visiting Chattanooga once, when their Uber driver asked them where they were from. My buddy replies, "Crossville" (which is 80 miles away, and not a major metropolis). The Uber driver then says "Crossville? Do you know that guy from Express Lunch who remembers everybody's name?" My buddy said they looked at each other in total shock. I was totally stunned as well. I can't personally think of anyone I know in Chattanooga. How does this Uber driver know about some sandwich servant in little ol Crossville, TN? This story taught me if we remember others first, they'll remember us.

This last July, I was dining out with my family. Our server, Melody, who was working and sweating very hard, thanked me for remembering her name, and said no one had ever called her by her name before. Melody wasn't thanking me for remembering her name; she was thanking me for caring enough about her to learn her name. Melody had confirmed the same feelings I had always had as a limo driver. We all want someone to care about us. Hmmm. Who's gonna care about us any more than the One who created us?

Man has his own textbook for how we do everything. The best thing to do is read man's textbook from cover to cover, know what it says, and throw it out the nearest window you can find. It's not a "one-size-fits-all" world. I've had to watch the man in the mirror for 54 years so far, and he's done a lot of not-so-smart things. My daughter once asked, "Dad, why am I always doing dumb things?" I said, "Yesterday, I did something not smart. Today, I did something not smart, and tomorrow, I'm probably gonna do something not smart. I'm just trying real hard to keep it to a minimum." This is why I try my hardest to let God be God, and let Him make all of my decisions for me. **Jeremiah 29:11: "For I know the thoughts that I think toward you, saith the Lord, thoughts of peace, and not of evil, to give you an expected end."**

How does man do marketing? Most everyone in this world wants to flock to social media. Would you rather have 1,000 "internet friends" or one REAL FRIEND who will NEVER leave you? That one real Friend can network better than any of us can. I personally do not have any social media accounts. I heard there was some kind of Express Lunch exposure on the Internet, but I didn't have anything to do with it. We do not advertise. It would be lack of faith or trust if we were to advertise, since Express Lunch is surrendered to the ultimate Networker of all time. I remind the staff that if we're doing our job right, people will come back. Thank you, Lord, for blessing us way beyond our imagination.

I read once where a restaurant owner is not supposed to give away any product to friends, because they will repeatedly abuse the privilege of free food, and could potentially put you out of business. A real friend is gonna wanna support you, and see you succeed. If the almighty lays it on my heart to extend gratitude, I have to obey. We have a large senior population in our area. Way too frequently, retired regulars will come in for the first time without their spouse who has recently moved on from this world, and it tears me apart. If God lays it on my heart after the death of a loved one, there's no way I can charge someone money. When someone is good to me, I have to reciprocate in the best way that I can. **2 Corinthians 9:7: "Every man according as he purposeth in his heart, so let him give; not grudgingly, or of necessity: for God loveth a cheerful giver."**

*Here's a cheerful giver. Jon Kraus from Silvara Stone*
*giving Express Lunch a new custom countertop.*

Recently, we had an individual we'll call "Mr. Dud" come in for the first time. Mr. Dud enlightened me on how he had a hot dog stand empire in Atlanta, and how we needed to start selling hot dogs at Express Lunch. **John 5:31: "If I bear witness of myself, my witness is not true."** Mr. Dud had been coming in every day for about a week, when he arrived holding an approximately 2 inch long green colored crafts type pencil that he said his wife found in the bottom of her salad. Well, it's ONE OF the craziest things I've ever heard, because we only have ink pens; no pencils on the property. So I'm totally at a loss for words with this little green colored lead pencil that was allegedly in the bottom of an eaten salad, but wasn't saturated with any dressing. Funny thing, but that baby was bone dry. While Mr. and Mrs. Dud were still in the parking lot eating their latest lunch purchase, I was informing our staff about what Mr. Dud had alleged. As you might guess, our staff had taken great personal offense to such allegations. I then headed out to the parking lot towards Mr. and Mrs. Dud's vehicle with my gravest "undertaker" persona. Picture John Carradine-Kung Fu's daddy. I informed Mr. and Mrs. Dud that I had thoroughly interrogated our entire staff, and was in "total dismay." I kept shaking my head, saying, "We don't even have any pencils on the property, let alone little green crafts pencils. Please accept my sincerest apologies (sure glad lightning didn't strike me), and next time you come into Express Lunch, please come real hungry, so I can take real good care of you." The very next morning, Mr. Dud was at Express Lunch by 10:30 a.m. to collect his free lunch. I've always told my children to be the bigger person, and of course, it's not always easy. We have to be the exception. **Proverbs 18:2: "A fool hath no delight in understanding, but that his heart may discover itself."**

We had a representative from one of our suppliers that we called the Queen of over promise, under deliver. She would say, "I'll bring your product on Monday." The only problem was, she never said which Monday. It could easily be two, three, or four Mondays away (or never at all) before we received what was promised. It would be a running joke when I would tell the staff that _____ (the representative) says she'll be by on Thursday with something we're really wanting, and all of the staff members would reply in unison, "Which Thursday?!" Call a "professional" to come to your house sometime to do a quote. See how many times these individuals promise to come out, and see if they ever show up. My dad always said, "If you're gonna do somethin', do it right." If you can ever get one of these folks to show up, do they then do the job right? Lots of people will come into Express Lunch for the first time saying that their friend said it was a really good place to eat. I always say "You'll never hear it from me; I have to under promise, and over deliver." **Proverbs 27:2: "Let another man praise thee, and not thine own mouth; a stranger, and not thine own lips."** What percentage of the time do we over promise and under deliver in this world? What a great OPPORTUNITY to be the exception!

A fellow I played music with in church was a manager of a franchised restaurant, and tried playing contemporary Christian music in this particular establishment one day. After just that one day, "an old lady" called their corporate office to complain, and this franchised location was no longer permitted to play Christian music. Knowing this story prior to purchasing Express Lunch, it was very important to me that we play Christian music. We, as Americans, get the freedom to stand up for whatever is right. I would be an ingrate if I didn't stand up for Jesus every day I'm on earth. I always thought if that "old lady" ever came in to complain, I would tell her, "Ma'am, please call the CEO of our company, He would love to hear from you." **1 Thessalonians: 5:17: "Pray without ceasing."**

*My daily walk brother Tommy Greer. He comes by Express Lunch virtually every day, and we play music together every Sunday morning at Meridian Church. Tommy is like a dad to our staff.*

Over the years, we have received a lot of compliments regarding the Christian music we play at Express Lunch, and I say to folks, "If we're ashamed of Him, He'll be ashamed of us." Being my first time as a restaurant custodian, I thought we would receive far more complaints of every nature than we do. Since the place is surrendered, it is also anointed. Every day is like a family reunion, and we never know who's gonna come through that door. Everything we do, down to the music we play, has to be the exception. That's why they call it "pop music," to describe what is gonna be most popular for those who are of this world. Everybody else can play "pop" music. As for me and my house, we're gonna serve the Lord.

*Another family reunion with Johnny Mac and Johnny R from Flipfest Gymnastics Camp.*

When man writes a book, what's the first thing he does? He has to proudly put his name on the front cover. On the back cover, man puts his picture, preferably with glasses and a pipe, to make himself look smart. Beneath the posed picture will be his extensive credentials, numerous college degrees, and diplomas from Oxford and Cambridge because he got too big for his domestic britches. If Your Servant ever wrote a book, hypothetical scenario of course ("wink wink"), he would humbly put "Your Servant" on the cover, and leave the rest to the Lord.

# CUSTOMER SERVICE

I really never gave this subject much thought until after purchasing Express Lunch. CEOs, managers, and business owners kept coming up to me saying they wanted me to come speak to their staff. It wasn't until the first CEO invited me to hang with her staff that I really thought about the secret recipe for customer service that we'll eventually discuss. Because everything is sales, every customer service representative has to sell themselves to the customer. Over 3 million people are employed as customer service representatives in the United States. An additional 1.65 million people are employed as sales representatives in the United States. Every sales representative is responsible for providing varying degrees of customer service before, during, and after the sale. There are 32.5 million businesses in the United States. Many businesses have more than one owner. All of these business owners are responsible for the proper care of their customers. Combined, this is a very large number. Add in the total number of employees from these 32.5 million businesses who perform some sort of service for their customers. Almost all of us perform some sort of customer service. Here's an example: picture Cooter from The Dukes of Hazzard saying "I'm a mechanic; what does customer service have to do with me?" Well Mr. Cooter, whose vehicle are you working on? The CUSTOMER'S! Because everything is sales, customers wouldn't have brought their vehicle to Cooter to begin with if they weren't sold on his automotive repair abilities.

How about those, for example, who are in a pastoral vocation? The pastor of a church, being a very good evangelist, has sold many people on The King of Kings. All of these people sold on Christ start attending the church where this pastor is a shepherd. The pastor of this church then has to follow up with the congregation (customers) to make sure everyone continues a Christ-centered life, and keeps returning to church (customer service). If the pastor doesn't provide proper customer service, everyone will quit coming to this church. Who then is left to fill the plate when it comes time to tithe? If there's nothing in the plate, there's no money to keep the lights on, and the pastor has no employment. Everything is sales, and a very large percentage of us have to learn all we can about how to follow up with proper customer service in the workplace.

Here's an even higher percentage: 100 % of us have to

deal with customer service representatives. How often are you impressed with what we call customer service? Do you dread having to deal with customer service representatives? How often do they get your order right at the fast food place drive throughs? When you think of customer service, what do you think of? Calling an 800 number and the person who answers is from another country, and you can hardly understand anything they're saying? How about scouring a website where you purchased something? You need helpful information, and there's no "contact us," or phone number anywhere. How about when you're waiting in line at a brick and mortar retail outlet to return something? When your turn arrives, you ask the customer service representative how they're doing, and they say in an unenthusiastic monotone, "I'll be real good in 37 minutes, when I get to go home." This statement translates into: "I'd much rather be back at the house in my Lazy Boy with a remote in my hand than here having to help you." How do these folks always have it down to the minute as to when they get to go home? Boredom and apathy. Attitude is everything! Customer service affects all of us, and sales is everything. Whatever our vocation, we have to learn all we can about serving, helping, communicating, and just plain dealing with other people. Just like we have to learn all we can about driving a vehicle, so we don't hurt someone. Just like we have to learn all we can about automotive mechanics, so we can operate a safe vehicle for ourselves and our passengers. Just like we have to learn all we can about computers, so we can function in a world full of technology. Just like we have to learn all we can about effective communications for when we're out evangelizing in the great commission.

Wanna study some real good customer service? How bout my buddy, Darwin? No, not Darwin the "theorist," who was a self-proclaimed agnostic, married his cousin, and had it all figured out where we all came from. I'm talking about my friend, Darwin Scarlett, whose business is right across the street from Express Lunch. Darwin Scarlett has a used car lot, an auto body repair business, and a wrecker service. The man is not only smart, but well diversified. I have the greatest respect for Darwin, because he works around the clock. When I encountered a herd of deer the hard way with my van, the insurer wanted to "total" the vehicle, and not have it repaired. Darwin repaired the van to my total satisfaction.

The first day I saw Darwin drive a nice looking Chevy Silverado truck, I knew it was a good vehicle, simply because he bought it for his inventory. When I saw Darwin drive this truck for his personal use every day for over a month, I knew it was a really good vehicle. When Darwin permitted me to drive the Silverado truck over 150 miles to, around Knoxville, and back, I knew that the man I was dealing with was a good one. So when I asked Darwin for his bottom dollar out the door after taxes, no funny stuff, and no surprises price, I knew what I was getting. When we went in to pay for the vehicle, my wife said, 'Don't you wanna counter offer or look around somewhere else? I said, "No, it's Darwin." This was the first time I had ever not negotiated the price of a vehicle. Funny thing, when a few adjustments needed to be made on the vehicle after purchase, what do you think Darwin did? He made the adjustments. How much do you think he charged me for these adjustments? If your answer is "nothing," you're absolutely right – he charged me nothing! It came back to me with proper service. That's being the exception; that's doing what's not typical of everyone in our world. That's taking care of your customer! We have to UNDER PROMISE AND OVER DELIVER, because far too many of us in this world blow up big what we say we're gonna do, and subsequently nothing happens. More than once, I've said to Darwin Scarlett, "Ya know, it blows my mind; you're the squarest guy I know, and you run a used car business?" Not the typical stigma we're accustomed to with the used car business. Darwin Scarlett is the exception. I've never once heard Darwin bring up the subject of the Lord. He doesn't preach; he just PRACTICES!

Whenever available, we order tomatoes from our local University of Tennessee Agresearch. Their product can't be beaten, and they take really good care of us. We refer to our contact there as "Tomato Girl," because the name says it all. If we only need one box, she'll still make the trip to deliver that one box to us. If we need 3 boxes, she'll pre-sort the boxes from most ripe to least ripe. Tomato Girl knows how to take care of her customer by going above and beyond exceptionally.

# EYES, EARS, AND BRAIN

Ever notice how we almost always remember a face, but almost always forget a name? Ever notice how it's an ADD (attention deficit disorder) world, where we rarely remember anything? When I train new staff members, I'll ask "have you ever noticed how it's an ADD world, and we rarely remember anything?" The new hires will be like "yeah, why is that?" I'll then say, "It's because we never listened." The first thing I'll tell new trainees is 98% of this world, I can't do. The other 2%, you just have to trust me, because I'm gonna lay success in your lap. The very next thing I'll tell a new trainee is "the most important thing you'll ever do, yesterday, today, or tomorrow, is LISTEN!" **Romans 10:17: "So then faith cometh by hearing, and hearing by the word of God."**

I'll then ask the trainee "when we listen, do we listen with our ears, or our brain?" There's always a pause, and then the trainee will say "both!" They think this is some kind of trick question, so the trainee always wants to hedge their bets by saying "both!" I'll then say it's a real simple question, The Almighty gave us ears so we can actually hear what has actually been said. We can't listen with the brain, because the brain thinks it always has everything "all figured out." Then I'll ask the trainee "when it comes to seeing, do we see with our eyes, or do we see with our brain?" There'll be another pause, and thinking it's another trick question, the trainee will once again say "both!" I remind the trainee that The Almighty gave us eyes to see what has actually been set before us to be seen. We can't see with the brain either, because the brain thinks it always has everything all figured out. I then tell the trainee the next question is the easiest of all. "When it comes time to think, do we think with our brain, or do we think with our brain?" The trainees then will smile big, and I'll say "it's that easy." We're the ones who wanna turn everything into rocket science. As we mentioned earlier, only One took the nails for all, and only One defeated death, Amen! It's that easy! **Proverbs 18:13: "He that answereth a matter before he heareth it, it is folly and shame unto him."**

One time our building had a little electrical concern, and without electricity, we couldn't open up for a couple of days. We had a big and loud generator running out back with 2 electric company service trucks right by the building. I purposely parked Darwin's black beauty Silverado in front of the entrance so no one could get in. There was also a big sign on the entrance door saying that we hoped to reopen very soon, which was strategically placed right at average height eye level, so no one would miss it. I'm conditioned to always watch the reflection in the window of the business across the street, so I can see our customers when they arrive in the parking lot. This provides the opportunity to start loving customers up one side and down the other, way before they ever enter Express Lunch. During this little electrical concern, I would catch a lot of folks when they first parked, and hurry to greet them, in an effort to minimize their inconvenience. Not as many folks as normal would even get out of their cars, because it was REAL obvious that we weren't open.

It's right around noon time, and I'm inside Express Lunch talking to my wife. A lady whose name I could not tell you, walks by all of the strategically placed deterrents and comes inside. She's very intrigued, and slowly says "it's dark in here." Slowly guarding my sharp slithery serpent sinner's tongue, I softly say "yes ma'am." She looks around some more, and says "there's nobody here?" I take another slow, but thorough look see around the place, and slowly guarding my sharp slithery serpent sinner's tongue, reply "no ma'am." Finally, this lady asks, "Are you open?" I then look this lady directly in the eyes hoping to get her attention, and say, while I'm slowly guarding my sharp slithery serpent sinner's tongue, "No ma'am." Folks from around here would have said "Bless her heart." There's always gonna be times when we don't use eyes, ears, or brain, the way our Almighty creator intended. Since we had no electricity, we were running a power generator through the back door, which was open and not secure. I had to sleep on the hard ceramic tile floor at night, with my favorite Louisville Slugger and Savior by my side for all the security I would need. I wasn't rested, or showered, but remained at Express Lunch until we could get everyone back to work and feed our families. Sinner that I am, this situation had me feeling a whole lot more cranky than Christ-like. I'm very thankful the Lord held back my sharp slithery serpent sinner's tongue. **Psalm 141:3: "Set a watch, O Lord, before my mouth, keep the door of my lips."**

More than once, I've attended a local men's group of really great guys who get together once a week. They bake brownies, open up with an acoustic guitar folky faith song from the 60s or 70s, and then analyze the Bible 3 or 4 layers deep, so they can become Super Theologians. These really great guys are focusing on the brain. If this is your bag, hey great. The Word is, the Word was, and the Word will be. It's that simple. If we're always looking for a problem, we're always gonna find one. Without providing a remedy, or better solution, then we're all merely critics. So how about this, what if we all went out into the frontline trenches of

The Lord's Army, and served in The Great Commission evangelizing with real "Smashmouth Servitude" that can take souls from a temporary world into an Eternal One? **Proverbs 14:23: "In all labour there is profit: but the talk of the lips tendeth only to penury."** The easiest thing in this world is surrender, the hardest thing is figuring it out. We turn to every temporary vice this world has to offer, and the last thing we come to (Christ), is the first thing we should have turned to (Christ). Nobody ever said evangelism was gonna be easy. Is it better to focus on our brains and become academia nuts, or focus on our hearts and bring in souls? **Proverbs 4:23: "Keep thy heart with all diligence, for out of it are the issues of life."**

What we're now focusing on is the answer to the third training question: The Brain! Have you ever noticed how the brain always thinks it has everything "all figured out?" How many times do we think we know what's best for us, and The Lord shows us a better way? Every day we have to surrender our pride, our ego, our tongue, our agendas, and let go of our finite vision and abilities. We had an employee once who was proud of their college degree in communications. I once attempted to say to this person "can we look at that chicken noodle soup recipe together?" The individual abruptly snapped "just tell me whether to make a half batch or a full batch." I was just humbly attempting to communicate with this person, thinking two noggins are better than one. Guess what? That particular batch of chicken noodle soup, which normally is very popular, was the wateriest, chickenless, noodleless, batch that was ever served at Express Lunch. I've always said "you can't rationalize with the irrational," so I really never attempted to communicate again with that individual who was so proud of their communications degree. Ever notice how The Lord loves to teach us with irony? Ironically, the person with the communications degree was as poor a communicator as anyone ever employed at Express Lunch. **Romans 12:16: 'Be of the same mind one towards another. Mind not high things, but condescend to men of low estate. Be not wise in your own conceits."**

I've had a lot of drumming apprentices off and on as well over the last 30 something years, and you know who was the only student I never could teach? It was the one who already knew everything. I don't know if the person with the communications degree ever learned anything from the anointing that Express Lunch has to offer, but that individual taught me something. If you're better than everybody, you better be better than everybody. Of course, no human being is better than any other human being. The experience also reminded me that I need to continually remind the staff how we can never over communicate. I'm very thankful for all of the many colorful employees who have worked at Express Lunch. I decided a long time ago that I'm gonna love everybody. If I don't, I'm the one who misses out. **John 15: 12-13: "This is my commandment, That ye love one another, as I have loved you. Greater love hath no man than this, that a man lay down his life for his friends."**

Hearing with our ears, seeing with our eyes, and thinking with our brain, without letting the brain have everything all figured out, are very important recurring themes we have to be constantly mindful of. When our staff is taking an order, and we don't listen exactly to what is said, the order we turn in will be made incorrectly. If the staff member preparing the order doesn't read exactly what is on that ticket, someone's lunch will be made incorrectly. Folks of the flesh are not as forgiving as our Father. One bad "booboo" might run a customer (or customers) off forever. For this reason, I have to be very careful with the people who are brought in to work at Express Lunch.

When someone applies for a position, I always tell them to arrive at 2:05 for interviews; it's a great way to observe someone's listening skills. We're open 10-2 Monday through Saturday, so 2:05 is the best time for me to meet with someone. I will say this last sentence verbatim, and it's unimaginable the responses that I've received. When a prospective employee calls, the Express Lunch staff, which I refer to as the SWAT Team, will shake their heads every time they hear me have to repeat multiple times the 2:05 part. When I'm on these phone conversations, I've heard responses such as "I'll just come in at 10:30 before you get too busy," or "I'll come in at noon someday, since you're a lunch place." I'll never forget one time, I had to repeat the 2:05 meeting time 3 times over the phone. The job applicant ended up arriving at 12:50, and we were still very busy. There was even one prospect who asked if it was 2:05 "at night, or in the day?" We have a lot of people eat a late lunch at Express Lunch, but never 2:05 a.m.?

Let's study the person we'll call "Liza." Unemployment rates had been very low for quite some time, and the hiring pool was really shallow. I had already met with Liza, who managed to find the place at 2:05 for her interview. I'll never forget the day she arrived at 9am for her tryout. It was on a Friday, and the high temperature was only supposed to be 27 degrees. It was the coldest day of the year for Crossville, TN. When Liza arrived at the same door she had already entered before for her interview, she just stood at it without entering. I was inside, lookin' at her, lookin' at me. I felt real bad, not doing anything, but I had to just stand there and stare at her, to see if she had enough cognitive wherewithal to come in. After a while, she yells through the door "It's Liza." I continued to stare as long as I could, but I felt real bad, because it was 9am, and we were currently nowhere near the 27 degree high temperature for the day. When I couldn't take it any longer, I finally waved for her to come in. Liza's brain had it all figured out that the door was locked, so she never even bothered to try the handle. The door was unlocked the whole time! Later, when one of Liza's pain pills bounced off the floor of the kitchen, she popped it in her mouth, and the tryout was over. Once I knew she wasn't feeling any pain, I didn't feel so bad for all of the time she had spent left out in the cold. May she be freed of her addictions. May no one ever start the addiction process, because many will never stop. **John 8:36: "If the Son therefore shall make you free, ye shall be free indeed."**

As of writing, this morning, I'm in Kroger picking out produce when a fella comes up to me and asks where some kind of corn with a special kind of silk was? I said "man, I'm sorry, I don't know. I don't work here, I'm just here doing my shopping like you." I then asked Tony, an actual Kroger produce employee, if he could help the man. I was wearing a Chicago Cubs baseball hat and a stars and stripes T-Shirt. I don't own any Kroger uniform shirts or name badges, and I'm also wearing a pair of shorts. How do our brains have it all figured out that Kroger employees dress like me? Feels like we have to watch our brains constantly, to keep them from always having everything "all figured out."

Over the years, from time to time, we've had first time customers TELL us that they ordered chicken salad, and we gave them tuna salad. Why do they always TELL us, and not ASK us whether we gave them tuna, or chicken salad? Could they possibly have it all figured out? After an instant examination, I'll tell the customer that we gave them the proper chicken salad that they ordered. Many of us will continue to want to argue that the chicken salad is tuna salad. Life here is too short to argue. You cannot rationalize with the irrational. I smile, say "WOW," and take off running back to the counter because our REAL customer is in a line that is getting backed up! If somebody comes in for the first time, and they already know more than staff members who have been doing the job for years, that's NOT your customer. Notice the parallel between not going to win all customers, and how we're not going to win all souls? We still can never quit trying to win all souls. In sales, we have to say "next," and move on to those we hopefully can keep from perishing. **Galatians 6:9: And let us not be weary in well doing: for in due season we shall reap, if we faint not.**

I do wanna tell ya about two real sweet ladies, one of which came to the counter, and asked me, instead of TELLING me, to come to their table. Simply telling this story just reminded me about the time a lady whistled for me to come to her table like I was a dog. Nobody ever said it was gonna be easy. Upon arriving at the table where the two "real sweet ladies" were seated, they told me they didn't know what to do. They had ordered ranch dressing for their salads, and what they were given, and subsequently poured all over their salads was "bleu cheese." I felt horrible, I didn't know what to say, I didn't wanna hurt the two sweet ladies feelings, I didn't want these two sweet ladies to feel foolish. The two sweet ladies both had a little dressing left in each of their cups, and kept insisting very kindly and repeatedly that I try it. "Just dip your finger, just dip your finger" they kept saying. Funniest part was both of them kept waving their little pinkies, like that was the finger I was supposed to use when I tried their "bleu cheese" dressing. Well, I was under huge pressure. What was I gonna do? I felt horrible, I didn't know what to say. I didn't want to hurt the two sweet ladies' feelings. I didn't want these two sweet ladies to feel foolish. I finally took a deep breath, and with a sigh, surrendered apologetically and retreated softly by saying to the ladies, "Ladies, it can't be bleu cheese. We don't have any bleu cheese dressing."

Now how can one sweet lady take a bite of ranch dressing on her salad, and tell herself and her friend that it's bleu cheese. Then the lady she's having lunch with, takes a big ol bite of ranch dressing on her salad and says "it is, it is bleu cheese." These ladies were so nice, they didn't wanna hurt my feelings, and I didn't wanna hurt theirs. Any guess as to how many times over the last 6+ years that our best-selling ranch dressing has been mistaken for bleu cheese? That's right, never. There's a first time for everything. How in this world (maybe that says it all), did these two sweet ladies become the first 2 customers ever to figure that one out? The mind is a VERY powerful thing. Have you ever seen someone tell themselves something that NEVER happened over and over enough times, until they finally believe a total fictitious fabrication actually happened? I've seen this delusional practice destroy multiple families. Seeing and hearing with the brain can be very dangerous, and as witnessed, does not discriminate between "nice" and "not-so-nice" people. That's why we all have to see and hear the truth. There's only one Truth, and we have to live for that Truth. **John 8:32: "And ye shall know the truth, and the truth shall make you free."**

Don't ya just love the one from man's textbook that says "the customer is always right?" The customer is not always right. If somebody thinks they're always right, they ain't your customer! Only God Almighty is the Only One who is always right! NO, the customer is not always right. Please respect me for having the courage to say that not everyone is your customer. When we're on the front lines in the great commission doing our job, we find out real fast that there are two kinds of people: those who get it, and those who don't. We're not gonna win em all. **Matthew 22:14: "For many are called, but few are chosen."** Even though we wanna be all things to all people, we've gotta focus on our studs, not our duds. You know who is the master of focusing on studs? A lil feller named satan. This is one very tough customer who knows his customer. Satan doesn't come after those who are consumed with a life of sin. He already has them. If we desire to stand up for Jesus with everything we have, satan will do anything he can to take our legs out from under us and make us his customer. **Matthew 7:13-14: "Enter ye in at the strait gate: for wide is the gate, and broad is the way, that leadeth to destruction, and many there be which go in thereat: Because strait is the gate, and narrow is the way, which leadeth unto life, and few there be that find it."**

Ever heard the one about the CEO who had it all figured out, by proclaiming "the internet was just a fad?" This story doesn't have the most prosperous ending, especially for a lot of innocent and loyal employees who ultimately lost their jobs. WHAT IF the CEO in this scenario was wrong? WHAT IF the CEO had slightly embraced the internet with minimal initial "toe dipping" exposure, just in case he was wrong? What if, after humbly admitting he was initially wrong, he was fluid enough to then put the pedal to the metal with internet exposure, so this particular story could have had a happier ending? What if we don't offer a possible solution? Then we're merely critics. **1 Chronicles 16:11; "Seek the Lord and his strength, seek his face continually."**

Let me ask you a foolish question: Have you ever been wrong? Every day at Express Lunch, we pack a large cooler with fresh sandwiches and salads that can't be sold the next day. Product waste can be very costly. I need a crystal ball to determine what to put in this cooler. WHAT IF it's a very nice day where everybody comes in? What if it's a very nice day where everybody goes to the lake, and doesn't come in? What if it's supposed to rain a sideways monsoon and nobody comes in, or just a light shower where we still get blessed abundantly with business? I'll often say to the staff "I'm gonna go with the odds, but whatever I do, it'll be wrong." I then shake my head, smile, and keep on truckin'. We can never forget how finite our vision and abilities are, and always keep everything surrendered to the One who repeatedly defies the odds like no other can. So very often, we have to ask WHAT IF? I'll say to the staff "2 things are for sure, we'll never make the Forbes 400, and we can never afford to allow this place to become insolvent and go under." WE ALWAYS HAVE TO ASK, "WHAT IF?!

## • • • •
# WHAT IF EVERYTHING WE SAY IS WRONG?

What if everything we say is wrong? Watch how we say everything so homogeneously in this world. How about our "no problem" example? For years now, most everyone thinks they love saying "no problem." 20-30+ years ago, our homogeneous world wore out the word "awesome." It was always used in an overly dramatic context. Let's say in an 80's valley girl voice: "how awesome, they have my favorite flavor of jelly bellies! Isn't that awesome?" Why would you ever wanna be like everyone else? The whole time, I was thinking there's only One who is worthy of the word "Awesome," and why would it be used in the context of this world? Eventually, our culture even got sick of saying and hearing "awesome," and we moved on to the word "amazing." **Revelation 3:16: "So then**

**because thou art lukewarm, and neither cold nor hot, I will spue thee out of my mouth.**" The overuse of the word "amazing" was so lukewarm at best, we even got tired of spewing it out of our own mouths. How can we make a hot as fire impression upon the world with lukewarm word usage?

So here we are in the year 2020. We've worked our way to everyone saying "no problem" everywhere we go. The best examples are when we're a customer in a retail outlet, restaurant, or financial institution. The customer hands a clerk or representative money for a product or service. The employer is paying that representative to stand there and take the customer's money. How more fundamental can that be? Where in any way, shape, or form, could there have ever potentially been a "PROBLEM?" How many times at these types of locations is the customer the first one, or the only one, to ever say "THANK YOU?" Then the retail establishment's representative replies "no problem." I hope it was "no problem," because all the paid representative has done all day is sit or stand there all day saying "no problem." The only time I wanna hear the words "no problem" are when I'm sunnin' my belly on a Jamaican beach, and a native Jamaican hands me a very refreshing beverage. I say "thanks, man," and the native Jamaican says in his native dialect "no problem, mon."

The problem with "no problem" is we have to understand where the $ comes from to begin with. When I'm blessed with a new trainee at Express Lunch who has come from a franchised fast food establishment, I'll ask them where the paycheck comes from. On more than one occasion, has the reply been "the manager." How many of us have any idea where the $ comes from? We have to first thoroughly understand that every penny comes from THE CUSTOMER! When I go to the grocery store, bank, or anywhere that I hand someone money, I always have to remind myself not to say thank you immediately, because I'm curious to see if anyone will ever say thank you at all on the other end. Many times, these cashiers hand me my credit card or change, and say "here ya go," with no thanks or sign of gratitude at all for helping provide them with a job. **1 Thessalonians 5:18: 'Give thanks in all circumstances; for this is the will of God in Christ Jesus for you."**

When we are children, we are supposed to be taught to say "thank you." Please observe how many of us say "thank you." This way, your own eyes and ears can make a very accurate determination. If you want to succeed at sticking out from the homogenous herd by being the EXCEPTION? Say THANK YOU! The greatest sales manual of all time says "in everything give thanks," so we have to give thanks without ceasing. At Express Lunch, when people say "thank you" to me, I keep finding myself saying "thank you" in return. Since man's custom is to reply with "you're welcome," I never say "you're welcome." The customer just helped me feed my family; what else can I say but "thank you?" Why is it that the customer is the one always thanking us for feeding their family, when ironically, the customer is the one feeding our families?

Nothing against the banking industry. I have some good friends in the banking industry, and they aren't the ones who make the rules. Why is it when we give the teller our money to deposit into their "institution," we're the ones thanking them? Isn't an "institution" the place where they put folks who need help in the head? The bank gives us zero point nothin' nothin' for our $, but if we want $ from them, they charge us how large of a percentage rate? I read recently where the average credit card interest rate is 16%. I can't imagine what blessings would be like at Express Lunch, if our margins were like financial institutions. The only debt I wanna owe is not to man, but to our Savior. Now there's someone to thank without ceasing. **Romans 13:8: "Owe no man anything, but to love one another: for he that loveth another hath fulfilled the law."**

*Another gift from my banker buddy Joe Salvato.*

Back when I was a kid, my grandpa used to always say "to tell you the truth," and it was always the truth. When I moved to the cities, especially on music row in Nashville, if someone said "to tell you the truth," it most frequently meant the furthest thing from the truth was being pitched towards me. Whenever someone says "to be honest with ya," I always say, or wanna say, "you mean you haven't been honest with me the whole time we've been talkin' so far?" To this day, I can't believe how many of us are still using "to be honest with ya." Quite often during prospective employee interviews, they'll say "to be honest with ya," and it spooks me every time. **Proverbs 12:22: Lying lips are an abomination to the Lord: but they that deal truly are his delight.**

I really don't get when so many of us wear out the saying "I could care less," when trying to prove the point that we don't care about something. If we could care less, that means we could care less, meaning we have to care to some degree, to be able to care any amount less. If we "couldn't care less," it means that we don't care at all. It's that simple; nothin' from nothin' leaves nothin'. The saying originally started out correctly as "couldn't care less," and we have said it incorrectly for so many years now that even Webster's dictionary now recognizes the incorrect saying. I've heard "could care less" used incorrectly in so many songs, movies, TV shows and speeches, that I'm staying far away from both the correct, and incorrect way of saying it.

When we first moved to Crossville, people kept saying "you need to come to "our" church," or "yuns need to come to "my" church." Why don't we ever say "wanna come to God's church?" Everything is His? For years, our society has had a saying "sex sells." There's nothin' more beautiful than a real Jesus girl who loves the Lord more than anything. Let's get as many beautiful Jesus girls out in the trenches selling salvation as we can! **Matthew 22:9: "Go ye therefore** into the highways, and as many as ye shall find, bid to the marriage." In our society, we say the employer is the boss, and the employee works for the employer. At Express Lunch, I tell everyone that I work for the staff, because if I can't keep them happy, they'll leave me. We have to be the exception. How about what we call "reality TV?" Nuff said? Can we do better? Most people call Express Lunch "Lunch Express." The other day, we had a group order for some teachers, and exactly 75% of the teachers wrote "Lunch Express" on their envelopes. Ever heard anybody say, "There are no stupid questions?" You kiddin' me? My wife can tell you that I ask stupid questions all the time. You know why? I wasn't listening. You know why I wasn't listening? It's an ADD world! Merely being accountable. **Romans 14:12: "So then every one of us shall give account of himself to God."**

When man "uses" someone, what comes to mind? Ever been used in a way those who are of this world sometimes use people? Of course, I'm using the term "used" as in being taken advantage of by someone. Does that make you feel good? Ever been used by the Lord? No greater privilege, huh? He'll use us all the time, if we let Him. Ever known anybody who "uses" the Lord? Scary stuff, huh? Lord, please use us in Your way, and never in ours. **Proverbs 10:9: "Whoever walks in integrity walks securely, but he who makes his ways crooked will be found out."**

Ever go into a grocery store where an employee is

consuming a really large portion of the aisle with this multi-level rig on wheels they are filling up for online grocery orders? When you, the customer, attempt to get around this rolling apparatus, you say "excuse me," or "I'm sorry, I'll get out of your way." The store employee then says "you're good." "You're good?" The customer is more than good, the customer is GOLD! The customer is Money in the Baaaaaank (John Anderson voice). The customer is the only thing that gives these employees a PAYCHECK! "Hmm? No customer, no paycheck; why me not get it?" (caveman voice) We're better than this! For any one of us human beings out there who still might be thinkin' about, possibly thinkin' about, maybe even starting to ever possibly think about, asking the question, "What does customer service have to do with me," I'll give you one word: MANNERS! We all must have manners. I get so frustrated when I'm attempting to maneuver through a very busy Express Lunch, and I get in the way of the customer. I'll always say, "I'm very sorry to be in your way." Of course, we've had staff who'll say "you're good," when they're the ones in the way of the customer. I'll just smile, look at the staff member without saying a word, and think wow, we don't get it. I have to pick my battles. Whatever happened to "please excuse me ma'am," or "please excuse me sir?" That's OPPORTUNITY, and I'm takin this OPPORTUNITY every time I can, by saying "PLEASE EXCUSE ME." There's ALWAYS A POSITIVE! **Luke 6:31:**

**"And as ye would that men should do to you, do ye also to them likewise."**

For years now, when we go into, or drive through a franchised food location, we're asked if we wanna "super size" something, or if we wanna add something to our order. Our society calls this "the upsell", and we almost always do it wrong. Everybody thinks they wanna ask for the "upsell" with a closed-ended question such as "wanna supersize those fries?" With a closed- ended question, the customer can only respond with a "yes" or a "no" answer. The problem is that we in our society, have been conditioned from birth to love saying the word "no." When we were infants, mama said "no, don't climb on that chair, you might fall." "No, don't touch that hot stove, you might get burned." Then after 2 years of always hearing the word "no" from mama, we turn "the terrible twos," and mama asks us to pick up our toys. We then challenge mama with a very defiant response of "NO MAMA!" Try being a short dumpy guy in school askin' a good looking girl for a date, and find out how much members of our society love saying the word "no." So guess what? Don't ever ask a closed-ended question, unless you are wanting the response to be "no." Think about how many times someone has asked you "want fries with that...no?" "Want a drink with that...no? "Want a hot apple pie with that...no?" The person asking these questions incorrectly is so proud of themselves, because they weren't afraid to ask for the upsell. The problem is, these questions were asked incorrectly, and without any real technique. In addition to the closed-ended kamikaze question, why would you shoot yourself in the foot by asking in singular form for just one drink, fries, or apple pie? If we "rev" back from half court, the ball might accidentally go in every blue moon, but what if we actually applied real techniques such as those used in shooting "free throws" or "layups", which produce a much higher accuracy of success?" **Proverbs 27:17: "Iron sharpeneth iron; so a man sharpeneth the countenance of his friend."**

At Express Lunch, we refer to what man calls the "upsell" as "the shoppin' list," and here's why. As a male, when I go into a store, do I carry a shoppin' list? Do I always walk out with everything I was supposed to walk out with? But I'm a male, why would I carry a shoppin' list? When a customer sets a chicken salad sandwich on the counter, I'll go down the list of potential accompanying items that we offer by saying, "How many cold drinks, hot soups, chips, cookies would you like? You would be surprised how many people will then say, "Oh, I forgot my Mountain Dew," or "I forgot my chips," and they then thank us. We're merely trying to help our fellow members of an ADD world not forget their favorite drink, snack, or goodies. Did you notice the "how many" part on the front end of the "shoppin' list," as opposed to the singular thought process used in the closed-ended "upsell?" I entered this world at 9 pounds, 9 ounces, and I've never been emaciated since. Ask me "how many " chocolate chip cookies I would like, and I'll tell ya give me a dozen, and a jug a milk to wash em down with. I've had many customers state virtually the same thing, and then say "Well, I'm feeling a little naughty today, I'll get a pack of cookies." Picture Ferris Bueller's high school office secretary, played by Edie McClurg, saying that last quote. Lots of times, customers will grab handfuls of cookies after they've been asked "how many" they would like. Now ask yourself "how many" cookies would have been moved without someone saying "how many?" You're planting the seed for multiple sales. "How many" souls would you like to see in heaven? GO FOR THEM ALL!

Just had a customer today add 5 bags of chips to a group order, and thank me very heartily for reminding her not to forget her chips. **NO ONE OWES US THEIR BUSINESS.** Actually, no one owes us anything. We're the ones who owe the debt. Making a living doesn't just happen automatically. We have to earn it with real technique. You would be surprised "how many" people say give me a bowl of chicken noodle soup for here, and 2 bowls to take home for later, when asked "how many bowls of soup would you like?" The same goes for multiple salads taken home for dinner that evening, or to be eaten in the next day or two, when a staff member properly plants the seed by asking the customer "how many" salads they would like. "How many" places do you go into, where the staff asks "how many" of something you would like? Exactly, that's why we do it. What an opportunity! We have to be the exception.

"How many" times do you go into a restaurant, and the individual who comes to your table says "Hi, I'm Ashley, and I'll be your server." Why is it no one has ever come up to your table and said "Hi, I'm Mike, your servant?" When people come into Express Lunch, I often greet them by saying "Welcome home," because I want folks to take tangible ownership of the place. If I think it's a first time customer, I'll ask a closed-ended "Been here before?" If it is their first time in, I want them to feel at home, and give them a quick tour, and introduce myself as Mike, "their servant." When people come to the counter to order for the first time, I tell folks "It's very fundamental here, you're the boss, and we're the servants." How many places tell the customer that they're the boss, and the staff is their servants? Exactly, that's why we do it. What an opportunity!

People ask me all the time where I go to church. I'll always ask "remember how Paul said we're supposed to pray without ceasing?" Why can't we go to church without ceasing? We've got more than two gathered, and the Lord's always here? Why can't we have church without ceasing? Why should we only have church on Sunday morning, and cheat ourselves from getting to celebrate our Savior all of the time?" I then tell people I play drums at "Meridian" every Sunday morning. How would man have answered the question "Where do you go to church? **Hebrews 10:24-25 : 'And let us consider one another to provoke unto love and to good works. Not forsaking the assembling of ourselves together, as the manner of some is; but exhorting one another: and so much the more, as ye see the day approaching."**

Multiple times daily, folks will call us to ask what the soups are for the day. What do we all wanna do? We want to answer the customer's question verbatim like "good little order takers." Picture Elmer J. Fudd saying that last quote. The most universal homogenous phone order taking example would be saying, in a very mundane absolutely non-charismatic totally apathetic monotone, "today we have Chicken Noodle Soup and Cheezy Chicken Taco Soup... no problem." This is why we have to be ever cognizant that EVERYTHING IS SALES! More times than not, when someone calls to inquire about our daily soups, they will ask "what kind of soup do you have today?" I always reply with "we have yummy soup today!" Then I'll say "we have Chicken Noodle Soup and Cheezy Chicken Taco Soup. How many bowls can I save ya!?" Why do I do this with such energy and excitement? Because ENTHUSIASM SELLS! It's our job to put the **F** into fun! Is the caller ever gonna come into the restaurant if they feel like they've mistakenly called a mortuary? Why do I ask how many bowls I can save for someone? Because I don't want the soup to sell out, and the customer to miss out, and URGENCY IS SALES! Most importantly, EVERYTHING IS SALES! Do we want anyone to miss out on the Kingdom of Heaven? I hope there are many parallels we can relate to our evangelistic walk.

A few days ago, one of our food suppliers had delivered two boxes of cheese to us that belonged to another restaurant. When the "owner" of this other establishment arrived, and asked us to carry out her boxes for her, and place them in her vehicle, she asked me "if I owned this place?" To properly illustrate, use Charlie Brown's teacher's voice for that last quote. Of course, I said that "The Lord owns this place." After a long pause, this restaurant "owner," who is well into her 70s, says..."ooooooookay?" She then says, "So do you pay the bills?" I replied, "No ma'am, the customer does." We were obviously having "a failure to communicate." Picture Strother Martin from Cool Hand Luke saying that last quote. She then proudly states that she is the owner of the other restaurant, and that it was the food rep's fault that the two boxes of cheese were delivered to Express Lunch. Our staff member and I didn't complain or place blame. This brief moment was no big deal to us, but in an effort to keep learning and growing, this incident caused me to ponder some questions. I wonder how we can breathe air for 70 years or more, and not have any idea Who owns everything?

Which makes me think, how many business proprietors are out there wanting to "boss" other human beings? How many employees are in suppressed work environments? Whether they were staff members, or drum students, I have always felt it was my job to empower others, not overpower others. **1 Thessalonians 5:11: "Wherefore comfort yourselves together, and edify one another, even as also ye do."** I've always tried real hard to say my statements to staff members in question form, hoping to stimulate thought, and humbly not parade myself as an expert. Asking staff members in question form also gives them the feeling of inclusion in decision-making processes. I have to ask a lot of questions. I sure don't know all the answers, but try real hard to work for the One who does. Lord, may all know who you are, and wanna live for you. **Matthew 6:33: "But seek ye first the kingdom of God, and his righteousness; and all these things shall be added unto you."**

We can never tell our family members enough that we love them. It's really hard for me to tell anyone else that I love them. If I've properly done my job as a servant, those around me will know that I love them without me audibly having to say it. When we're blessed with a staff member who comes to work, to come to work, versus those in the past coming to work, to stand and talk, I will nurture and groom them to the best of my ability. Regretfully, over the years, we've had personnel who have been on the clock, and off of the clock all at the same time. When I take the time to convey all of the many things I've had to learn the hard way at Express Lunch with a staff member who knows how to bust tail, and wants to learn, I always end with "you know why we had this conversation?" The prized employee will then say "because I'm worth it." They know what answer to give, because I've told them numerous times they're "worth it." Do you like knowing you're worth something? The best thing we can tell someone is "I BELIEVE IN YOU." Lord, thank you for being the King of Kings, and the greatest of all to believe in.

*Rachel, Dani, Tosha, and Jessie from our SWAT Team(Sisters With A Tremendous toughness). Not pictured are Jaz, Mel, Kelsey, Tian, and 2 more additions arriving next week. Thank you Lord for our staff!*

Our society has called Elvis "the king," Richard Petty "the king," Michael Jackson, "the king of pop," Muhammad Ali (Cassius Clay) repeatedly called himself "the greatest." Kobe Bryant said he was "the greatest." Of course, the captain of the Titanic said that "not even God himself could sink this ship." We have to be very careful with the words we use as a society. The excessive praise we often express towards others can also contribute largely to "stars" thinking they're bigger than life. Brad Paisley has a really good song example where the lyrics say, "When you're a celebrity, it's adios reality." It's one of my favorite songs, and well worth a listen. Humility is an exceptional trait that cannot be overlooked. **Luke 14:11: "For whosoever exalteth himself shall be abased; and he that humbleth himself shall be exalted."**

Twelve years ago, I sat next to a lady on an airplane who looked to be somewhere between 80-90 years old. It was presidential election time, and her first question to me is are you red or blue? I immediately looked her in the eye and kindly said, "I'm both, with a whole lot of white in the middle." I had never been asked that question before, but why would rehearsal be necessary? We're Americans – shouldn't we all be red, white, and blue? Whenever someone asks me which political party I belong to, I always say SERVANT. What if saying we were republicans was wrong? What if saying we were democrats was wrong? **Mark 3:25: "And if a house be divided against itself, that house cannot stand."** What if we all said we were from the "American Party?" What if we all pledged allegiance to The United States of America? What if we all were one nation under God? What if we all were indivisible? What if there was Justice for all in one big American Party? What a party it would be if we all simply got along. What if, instead of running around like a bunch of elephants and donkeys, we went into all of the nations as servants? When Jesus spoke, did he tell everyone present that they all needed to be divided into groups far apart from each other? "Now we need the Theseodists to sit over here, the Themodists to sit over there, and the Thoseodists to sit way back over yonder."

> **1 Corinthians 1:10: 'Now I beseech you, brethren, by the name of our Lord Jesus Christ, that ye all speak the same thing, and that there be no divisions among you; but that ye be perfectly joined together in the same mind and in the same judgment.**

How's this for getting along? The other day, the Louie family from Virginia came into Express Lunch for the first time. They introduced themselves as Louie, his current wife, his former wife, and his daughter. Mr. Louie said they spent every holiday together, and that's how they "get along." When I delivered two Reuben sandwiches to Mr. Louie and the current Mrs. Louie, she immediately offered half of her sandwich to the former Mrs. Louie. After studying how these two women interacted like best friends and sisters, I couldn't quit thinking about what an inspiration this family is, and what kind of person I'm supposed to be. I'm very thankful to have met these model examples of peaceable people. **Romans 14:19: "Let us therefore follow after the things which make for peace and things wherewith one may edify another."**

*Thank you Louie family for exemplifying how we should all get along.*

How about when we say Columbus discovered America in 1492? We had it all figured out, and then found out that this Columbus guy never stepped foot in North America.

Are we too proud to retract our booboo? How about when we say, or sing, "Here comes Peter Cottontail? What do colored eggs and chocolate bunnies have to do with our Savior's Resurrection? If we want to celebrate Jesus defeating death, why can't we celebrate a living Savior EVERY DAY, instead of on just one diluted day that confuses the actual event? How about when we say or sing, "Here comes Santa Claus, here comes Santa Claus?" Although I've always been extremely impressed with how Santa shimmies down each one of our chimneys in the mere course of just one night, there is no one who can compare with the miracles our Messiah has performed. I have to have the facts, so let's get the facts. I report, you decide. The real St. Nicholas came from the 3$^{rd}$ century, and gave away all of his wealth, so he could care for the poor and needy. What a great guy! We already celebrate St. Nicholas on December 6$^{th}$, which commemorates his death. I just never had any idea, until I got the facts. Santa can have all of the spotlight on December 6$^{th}$! If we already close all of the banks on Columbus day, when Columbus never actually did anything, can't we get all of my banker buddies another day off on December 6$^{th}$ to honor St Nicholas? We had it all figured out that Jesus was born on December 25$^{th}$. Now, as close as we can tell, Jesus was actually born 9 months later. "What if" we're wrong again? It's happened before? Let's make it real easy. Instead of confusing and diluting one day a year with Jesus' birth, let's celebrate the birth of our Savior EVERY DAY! If all of us can recognize the Savior with wrapped up presents at Christmas time, why can't we all live our lives for Him like He lived his life for us? Can you imagine what all of the critics would want to say about Santa and all of his presents being eliminated from CHRISTmas? Picture Festus Haggen from "Gunsmoke" responding to the critics with, "Now shut yer tater trap, quit all that slackjaw, and bend yer ear this a way. This here chubby lil ol servant feller ain a tryin' to get rid a Santy Claus, he's just a tryin' to get ya to focus on the only thing that really matters: The Greatest Gift of all: Jesus Christ! **Psalm 86:12: "I will praise thee, O Lord my God, with all my heart: and I will glorify thy name for evermore."**

Of all the things we say in our society, our greatest OPPORTUNITY lies within what we call customer service. Have you ever noticed how every single one of us is a servant? We're either serving others, or we're serving ourselves. Is it better to serve man, or serve The Lord? Customer service is serving the customer. Who is the customer? Man. CUSTOMER SERVITUDE is serving The King of Kings! There is none higher! The greatest sales manual of all time says we're to love the Lord our God with all our heart, with all our soul, and with all our mind. Until we love the Lord with all we've got, how can we ever learn how to love our customer properly? Customer Servitude gives us a Higher gear than mere man and his customer service can provide. If we love the Lord more than anything, we will serve humankind with everything. Man's customer service textbook says "customer first." Picture Paul Lynde saying "NO No No No Noooooo!" Try putting the Lord first. Give it a try, I dare ya! Nothing against man, but none of us ever took the nails for all, or defeated death. CUSTOMER SERVITUDE IS THE SECRET RECIPE FOR SUCCESS, AND OUR GREATEST OPPORTUNITY! **Colossians 3:23: "Whatever you do, work at it with all your heart, as working for the Lord, not for human masters." 1 John 4:8: "He that loveth not knoweth not God; for God is love."**

The greatest day Express Lunch ever had, has nothing to do with $. Mr. and Mrs. Betz would come in all of the time, and became like parents to me. Mr. Betz was taking chemo treatments, and having a hard time. Due to the treatments, there were times he would come in with his hair looking like Doc Brown in the movie "Back to the Future." I hated what he was going through. I knew Mr. and Mrs. Betz were from the northeast, but with every one of my subtle references to Jesus, they never participated in responding dialogue. One late afternoon, the timing was right. There were 10 of us total: 8 "Jesus people," all of whom I knew, and the Betzs. I went over to Mr. Betz and said "Mr. Betz, is it ok if we pray for you?" Mr. Betz, an old Navy man who served our country, complete with a salty sailor voice to prove it, replied, "Well,

I'll take all I can get." I'm not a hugger. Women wanna hug all the time, and I feel it's disrespectful to hug another man's woman. I try really hard to adhere to a "no touchy (David Spade/Emperor's New Groove voice)" policy. So because I'm not a hugger, I branch out and put my arm around Mr. Betz, who is seated. Even during the prayer, sinner that I am, I'd sneak a peek at Mr. Betz. His eyes and nose were just running away. The floodgates had been opened. After Mr. Betz's spiritual soaking, he says "I always knew there was somebody looking after me." There was not a dry eye in the house. Man, I loved that day. I was so thankful to be used. I never got to see Mr. Betz more than a couple of times after that. Mrs. Betz would come in a lot more times by herself, and every time I would wonder if Mr. Betz had moved on to bigger and better things. For the longest time, she would come in and say that Mr. Betz said, "I hate this hospital food; go see Mike." I can still hear that salty sailor voice like it was yesterday. Miss my old buddy; sure hope he's enjoying sailing the seas with The Savior. Praying with a man for his soul –how's that for priceless customer servitude?

# WE ARE ALL UNIQUELY CREATED

Man has said that there are 4 different personality types: **analyticals**, **drivers**, **amiables**, and **expressives**. The **analytical** is the one who wants all of the facts and figures, and is going to take their time getting the job done right the first time: The thinker. The **driver** is the one in charge, and wants solutions: The leader. **Amiables** are easy to get along with because they don't like conflict: The follower. The **expressive** is oftentimes the loudest in the crowd, and wants to be included in everything: The entertainer. Since communicating with others is one of the necessary skills identified that we need to learn all we can about, we have to also learn all we can about every type of uniquely created personality that is in this world. If we're out in the trenches doing our evangelistic job, we have to know what we've got, and what we're dealing with. Since everything is sales, how do you sell these four types of personalities? In most of my sales experiences, I was calling on business owners and key decision makers, which meant I was primarily dealing with drivers who don't want to work for someone else. A sales professional has to be a very good chameleon, and adapt to any personality in front of them. With drivers, I would oftentimes humbly do my "Gomer" persona, which would allow the driver to think all of my proposals were "their idea." The amiable simply needed their hand held, and to be reassured that they were doing the right thing. Conversation with the analytical had to be controlled with just the high points taken from fundamental facts. If the analytical starts asking a barrage of questions, they can really beat you to death. With the expressive, we are doing them a great disservice if we allow them to miss out on what "everyone else" is doing.

There's only one problem with man's 4 personality types; there's far more than just four of them. The Maker of Heaven and Earth can create anything He wants, anytime He wants, and any way He wants! Here's a few examples that merely a simple servant like me has encountered over the years, how to handle them, how to help them, how to cope with them, and how NOT to be them:

**<u>Little Big Man</u>**- When I was chauffeuring in Nashville, there were a lot of airport pickups. The paperwork would always say meet the client at the gate, baggage, or ground terminals. If possible, I would meet the client at the gate as often as possible. This technique would provide for a greater opportunity to meet, and learn from all of the many people this world would call successful, because they had the $ to be traveling with special accommodations. Of course, the longer amount of time I spent with the clients carrying their luggage, and entertaining them with laughter, meant the greater the opportunity to earn a more plentiful subsequent happy ending of a gratuity. Hey, is it better to be a sinner, or a sinner who repents? A sinner who repents of course, because we're all sinners.

When assigned to pick up Little Big Man, my paperwork said to meet him at ground transportation. Since my previously scheduled ride brought me back to the airport barely in time for Little Big Man's scheduled arrival, I did exactly as the paperwork instructed. After waiting for what felt like forever, I suddenly heard all kinds of yelling and expletives from the top of the escalator for all of ground transportation at the Nashville International Airport to witness. This whole commotion is caused by a lil feller in his late 30s, who's kickin' and cussin' all of his luggage down the escalator, and yellin' to the whole world that he just had back surgery, and couldn't lift any of his luggage that I was supposed to be carrying for him. As servants frequently and humbly have to do, I took it off of him, and replied only with numerous apologies. When I finally got Little Big Man settled into his comfy limo, I did something I had never done before. I held out my ride assignment and said Mr. _____, "I did exactly as instructed." I didn't want to get anybody in trouble, but I had hoped now that Little Big Man didn't have such a great audience, that he might simmer down some. Little Big Man then called the Limo Company to show off some more of his back side, and make certain that his transportation accommodations were correct for the following three days that he was going to be in Nashville. He also informed the limo company that he wanted me to be his personal chauffeur for the duration of his stay. I guess he had figured out that I could take whatever he dished out.

Later that afternoon, we picked up Little Big Man's lady friend, which turned his disposition around. He now had to act like a nice guy in front of his woman. At the end of the three-day tour of duty, I dropped Little Big Man back off at the airport. He handed me his business card, which allowed me the chance to see that he was the CEO of a major company. He then offers me the position of being his full-time personal chauffeur in Philadelphia, PA. I was very flattered, but between Little Big Man's paltry gratuity and winter weather in Philly, I gratefully declined the full-time chauffeuring position. The person who wrote down the initial ride assignment for the Little

Big Man tour either didn't listen with his or her ears, didn't read with his or her eyes, or maybe both?

> **Proverbs 21:23: "Whoso keepeth his mouth and his tongue keepeth his soul from troubles." Proverbs 29:11: "A fool uttereth all his mind: but a wise man keepeth it in 'til afterwards."**

<u>Yosemite Sam</u>- Little big man with a very bad temper. Exemplified by Little Big Man kicking his luggage down the escalator at the airport complete with numerous expletives. There's no telling how many times I've been Yosemite Sam in the past. By God's grace, there's no telling how many times I now stop, take a deep breath, and say "what is the positive opportunity that you're trying to lay in my lap Lord?" There's always a positive, and we're in charge of our emotions. People don't make us mad; we allow them to make us mad. Temper is like swingin' the hammer at the fair, and dingin' the bell. It flies a direct beeline from the toes to the brain, and we've gotta stop it with a deep breath and surrender before somebody gets hurt. **James 1:19-20: "Wherefore, my beloved brethren, let every man be swift to hear, slow to speak, slow to wrath: For the wrath of man worketh not the righteousness of God."**

**Big Al (The Hitman)** - The personality we are calling Big Al and I were both sales representatives for a major corporation, and were transferred to improve the Eastern Tennessee region. My job was to perform and produce, and Big Al's new job was to be the new district manager. Big Al was an abrasive pusher, who no one in the Nashville region liked, with the exception of the big bosses, who enjoyed reaping the $ residual reaped from Big Al's efforts. I still made the transfer over with Big Al, because he had mentored me, and I had a family to feed. Good thing I adhered to an old adage brought to me while in Nashville. "Be careful of the toes you step on today, for they may lead to a part of the anatomy you'll have to kiss tomorrow." How was I to know that Big Al was eventually gonna be my boss? We always have to ask what if?

Our two most senior representatives in this new eastern region each had over 30 years with the company, and both were real good solid guys. One of these two good guys wasn't hitting "the number" any more, so Big Al performed a hit on him, and the first man with 30+years with this particular company disappeared. It broke my heart. The second representative was absolutely belittled in front of everyone in a district meeting. Big Al verbally pounded the man repeatedly. I thought this 60ish year old man was gonna cry, I thought I was gonna cry. I've never been convinced with how man does corporate

America? Talk about homogenous word usage, our corporate world is all gonna "reach out" and "engage" the customer with all of their "transparency." Where I come from, we just "get a hold of somebody, and see if we can help em out." There's always a positive, corporate homogenous lingo provides great OPPORTUNITY for those who wanna be the EXCEPTION! **Matthew 23:3: "All therefore whatsoever they bid you observe, that observe and do; but do not ye after their works: for they say, and do not."**

**Mr. Roboto**- Ever have somebody who's trying to sell you something, telemarketer, etc., say "how are you?" Before you even get the chance to reply, this sales charlatan is throwing their pitch at you. When somebody doesn't give you time to tell them how you are, or wanna listen to how you are, it's obvious they don't give a rip van winkle about ya. I'm already out at this point. If in doubt, stay out. We had an employee once who was a real good guy, but real stiff. Mr. Roboto was in his mid 20s, and supposedly had an associate's degree in Culinary Arts. The problem, or irony once again, was that Mr. Roboto was real sloppy in the kitchen and nobody wanted him back there. My only choice was to put Mr. Roboto on one of the front registers. Mr. Roboto had 2 lines in his repertoire. As folks walked in, he would say (in Dan Akroyd conehead voice) "Hi, how are you." I'm not putting a question mark at the end, because he wasn't asking anybody, he was just shpeelin it out like a robot. Sure makes ya feel warm and fuzzy doesn't it? As folks would leave, Mr. Roboto would whip out a heartfelt "Have a great day" (again in Dan Akroyd conehead voice). I can't ever remember personally using either one of those standard lines. I'll say "How ya been?" "You doin' good? or "You okay?" It's kinda like with my drum students. I'll ask em, "When you play the drums, do you think with your brain, or do you think with your heart?" If someone plays the drums with their heart, it flows and grooves a whole lot better. Same with customer interaction and communication. We've gotta flow from the heart, or we might end up sounding like Mr. Roboto.

**The Humble Servant** - This was my grandpa, whom I grew up with right next door to me on the farm. Unlike Big Al, this is how my grandpa took care of people. My grandpa told me that in the old days, when he needed help on the farm with hay balin' and such, he always paid the young guys he could round up more $ than any of the other farmers around. My grandpa said it came in real handy come Halloween, because he would be the only farmer around who never got his outhouse tipped over. I've worked with a lot of servants that fit this personality. They almost always smiled, and were soft spoken. These people know there is no greater privilege than to serve our Lord and Savior. Wise servants know to guard their tongue for now, because our true treasures wait in heaven. **Matthew 23:11: "But he that is greatest among you shall be your servant." Proverbs 16:23: "The heart of the wise teacheth his mouth, and addeth learning to his lips."**

<u>The Prayer Whisperer</u>- You know how the greatest sales manual of all time says we aren't supposed to covet our neighbor's house, spouse, or materials? Fortunately, I don't. I do have a great admiration for those folks who have the ability to express the most heartfelt eloquence when utilizing the personal hotline we all have to the Almighty. I am nowhere near the master of public prayer. In personal prayer, I try real hard not to be a jabbering gentile who is rattling off personal requests like a kid with a mile long Christmas gift wish list. When praying, I feel like it's my place to ask for nothing, and give thanks for everything. If I empty myself of me, and simply LISTEN, He'll tell me what He wants, and what's best for me. My wife is the prayer whisperer. Her prayers are weapons of mass salvation. She can penetrate hearts so deeply, it brings tough guys to tears.

*Marti K - The Prayer Whisperer*

**The Braggadocio**- This person is really proud of themselves. We recently had a new customer come in looking like Lord Farquhar from the movie "Shrek." This person immediately comes through the door, and introduces themself as "Colonel Robin" (retired military). I've never in my mere 54 years, ever had anyone introduce themselves with a title of anything! Yes, I'm very grateful for all who have fought for our freedoms. Just ask the military personnel who have been administering testing at our local health department this summer, and come into Express Lunch every day. Yes, I'm gonna love ya as I do myself, but I don't care if you're Colonel Batman, Colonel Klink, or Colonel Sanders. Believe me, I'm a very big fan of Colonel Sanders chicken. Hmmm, if I'm not impressed with any title of the flesh, imagine how unimpressed The Almighty will be, come judgement day, when someone tries to tell the Master that they were some kind of "superstar" during their temporary stay on earth. Ever look up how many references there are in the greatest sales manual of all time as to how we are not supposed to be prideful people? If we enable the behavior, we've done folks of this personality a disservice. Takes a lot of time and patience to bring these folks to the land of humility. We all have a hard time with pride. I know it's very cliché, but we've gotta "let go, and let God." **James 4:16: But now ye rejoice in your boastings: all such rejoicing is evil."**

*Thank you for your service.*

<u>Tarzan</u>- He's easy to spot. Tarzan is the guy who's so proud of himself; he's always beatin' his chest. **Proverbs 11:2: "When pride cometh, then cometh shame: but with the lowly is wisdom."**

<u>Loudest in the Crowd</u>- Ever notice how the loudest talker in the crowd is an expert in everything? I used to have to fly a lot, and the same guy would always be on the same plane with me. He would be about 3 or 4 rows behind me, and blow incessantly out of an orifice The Almighty never intended us to speak out of, because he couldn't help not to take full advantage of the captive audience. That dude made for a long sleepless flight every time. **Proverbs 10:19: "In the multitude of words there wanteth not sin: but he that refrained his lips is wise."**

<u>Large and in Charge Marge</u>- Much akin to the last character, the personality we are calling Marge used to yell across Express Lunch for all to hear about all of the things I was supposed to do to properly run the place. Haven't seen Marge in a few years. Good thing we let the Lord keep the place runnin' and open. **Proverbs 19:21: "There are many devices in a man's heart; nevertheless the counsel of the Lord, that shall stand."**

<u>Myron (or Myra) Monotone</u>- This is the guy who in the old days of courtship walked up to a girl's door with flowers and

a box of candy, and said in mundane Droopy Dog cartoon voice, "You wouldn't wanna go out with me, would you? I didn't think so," and walks away with a sunken head, and tail between his legs.

**Magic Mike**- This is the guy who goes up to the girl's door and says (in Vinnie Barbarino voice) "Yo, when do you wanna go out wit me, Friday night or Saturday night? Wait, you wanna go out wit me on Friday night, cuz this date ain't gonna end 'til Sunday mornin." I'll never forget one time when the CEO of a bank asked me to speak with her employees about customer servitude. I picked the most librarian-esque female in the crowd to run this scenario on. Afterward, I overheard the librarian-esque female tell the CEO that this guy was the best speaker they ever had! When properly utilized, the Magic Mike persona will take their breath away. There's a fine line between cockiness and confidence, and we have to be careful. Cockiness is a bad thing; confidence is everything. **1 John 4:4: Ye are of God, little children, and have overcome them: because greater is he that is in you, than he that is in the world.**

**Eeyore**- My buddy Eeyore moves real slow, and with a sideways swagger similar to a cowboy. Whenever we would walk anywhere, I would say "man, you cover more ground sideways than you do forwards." My buddy Eeyore is one of the most Blessed individuals I know, but he's always so busy telling me about how bad he's got it. He has no idea. Makes me hear Linda Ronstadt sing "Poor Poor Pitiful Me." **James 5:13: "Is any among you afflicted? Let him pray. Is any merry? Let him sing psalms."**

<u>Bummer Man</u>- Very similar to Eeyore. I couldn't tell ya the last time I went to see my buddy Bummer Man. You know why? Nobody wants to be around Bummer Man! It's our job to put the **F** into fun! As servant evangelists, we've gotta make people want what we have (Christ)! Remember the Movie "When Harry Met Sally," directed by Rob Reiner? There's a very memorable scene in a restaurant with Meg Ryan and Billy Crystal, where Rob Reiner's real life mom says, "I'll have what she's having." I know it's very cliché again, but it's still true and one of the best sayings there is: "Attitude is everything." **Proverbs 17:22: "A merry heart doeth good like a medicine: but a broken spirit drieth the bones."**

<u>The Rah Rah</u>- Exactly opposite of the last two personalities, the Rah Rah is the person who cheers "give 110 %!" Picture Misty Rowe from "Hee Haw" cheering that last quote. She did a good job, huh? There's only one problem; there's no such thing as 110 %. Anyone who has ever given every full ounce of themselves knows what 100 % is. There's no more

than 100 %, and most importantly, there's no less than 100%. As the best sales manual of all time says, whatever you do, do all to the glory of God.

**The Groupie**- Ever known somebody who always had a "friend" somewhere, or maybe everywhere? They're not only always at all the music concerts, they're at all the social events, or anywhere they can be seen. The groupie group largely consists of man's expressive and amiable (follower) personalities. The groupie sure wouldn't ever wanna "miss out" on anything. We have to be very careful not to follow the wrong crowd, or let our children follow the wrong crowd. **Proverbs 14:12: "There is a way which seemeth right unto a man, but the end thereof are the ways of death."**

**The Social Butterfly**- Might be the groupie's mom. Speaking of moms . . . .

**Mommie Dearest**- Example of large and in charge. Also an example of how we are not to be. Loves the control. Man's "driver" example. Their offspring either have no choice but to be their mom's "amiable," or they try to become just like the domineering parent as soon as they get the chance. Intercessory prayer for the parent and child is the best I can come up with. The Lord can always help better than anybody.

**The Queen of England**- Never met her, seems like a nice lady. Not really sure what she does for a living, or what she did to earn the gig, but pretty sure this world will still keep on turning whenever the time comes for her next chapter. The point is, no one is the queen of England, including the queen of England. Every blue moon, at Express Lunch, we encounter those who wanna think they're the queen of England, but only the King of Kings and Lord of Lords is worthy to be knelt before.

**The Queen Bee**- Now this one is not nice. We just simply have to refer to our observation that not everyone is our customer. We used to encounter a few of these in the early days where we killed 'em with kindness, and it was like water on a witch. This personality had to either become like us, or they just disappeared. We will not win 'em all. **Matthew 22:14: "For many are called, but few are chosen."**

**The Nag**- Picture Charlie Brown's teacher's voice. This is not your customer. Keep praying without ceasing.

**Miss Congeniality**- Exact opposite of the Queen Bee. In the south, she's the one who's always saying "bless your heart," which translates into "how in the world does this person I'm patronizing by saying 'bless your heart' to have enough cognitive horsepower to ever find their way out of their own driveway?"

**The Scorekeeper**- If you've ever said or done something once or twice, or maybe never even at all, the scorekeeper will repeatedly hammer you about how you've said or done this alleged vision of delusion 100 times. The scorekeeper will repeatedly accuse you of doing something they are actually doing. An example would be when the scorekeeper accuses a spouse of infidelity, when, in fact, the accuser has actually been the unfaithful one. The scorekeeper will tell you you're miserable, when you thought you were happy. The fact is, the scorekeeper is the one who's miserable. This is a very competitive person by nature, and there is "no win" with the scorekeeper always being the one who has to control the scoreboard. Man calls this behavior "deflecting." It's very twisted and messed up, so run as far and as fast as you can in the other direction when faced with a scorekeeper. Once again, intercessory prayer, and you can't rationalize with the irrational.

**Starin' Stella**- Ever seen somebody with a stare that said over medicated or under medicated? While once again in that familiar land of desperation, I found myself once again interviewing job applicants. When I sat down with the personality we are calling Starin Stella, she was talking up a big game. Starin' Stella said she had been a supervisor at a major food franchise for years, and let me know that she was gonna take a lot of the work load off of me by running the place for me. The most memorable part of the interview was when she told me she was a stickler for being punctual. Her quote was, "If you're fifteen minutes early, you're on time. If you're on time, you're late. If you're late, it's unacceptable." Take one guess what happened on Starin' Stella's third day. How did you get it? Starin' Stella was over 15 minutes late on her third day! Whenever any staff member comes in apologizing for being late, I always say, "Hey, it's all that much less I've gotta pay ya." There's always a positive.

In sales, you don't sell after the sale. Starin' Stella didn't have to keep blowin' herself up in the interview. I was desperate, and had to give her a tryout no matter what. Simply out of curiosity, I did want to see superstar Stella in action. After a very few days into her very short tenure, Starin' Stella had designed a custom public relations position for herself, where she was gonna "reach out" and "engage" her numerous networking contacts, and bring us tons more business. I attempted to enlighten Starin' Stella on how we were already blessed to capacity, and couldn't create this customized "PR" position for her. The news didn't go over well. Starin' Stella's knife wielding abilities during food prep became significantly more pronounced and aggressive, which caused me to have a "what if" vision. I got to thinking how many people I could try to help in this world while I'm lying face down on the kitchen floor with a knife fatally penetrating my back? I think my hands were shaking when I had to inform Starin' Stella that we were not gonna continue working together.

**The One Upper**- Ever know anybody who always thought they had to be better, or have everything that was better than everyone else? We had what man would call a textbook "narcissist" for 3 years, 2 months, and 14 days, come into Express Lunch virtually every day and "homestead" with his little backpack at a 4 top table. Since I was a captive audience, this lil big feller would stay until after 4 and 5 p.m. on multiple occasions so he could talk about how great he was. Remember how we close at 2 p.m.? If I ever got a word in, this individual would always "one up" me with how he could do better, or how he knew more. The most frustrating part? This charlatan was supposed to be a pastor of a local church. Not meaning to be a scorekeeper, but I don't ever remember him once referencing scripture. I guess why would he talk about Him, when he could talk about himself? I tried my best to help this person, but did not succeed. Look up narcissism – the chances of helping these folks are not the best. We have to be very careful. Most importantly, "WE'RE" BETTER THAN THIS, DOGGONE IT!

**The Expert**- Ever notice how sometimes we think we know everything? We've got to keep learning, growing, and serving every day! I'm always saying to the staff, "what are we gonna come across today, that we've never experienced before?" On the surface, to man, it's "just a sandwich shop." Every day, when people come through that door, we get to be reminded of invaluable life lessons we can carry with us, and pass on to others. Some days we learn what to do, and other days we learn what NOT to do. **Romans 1:22: Professing themselves to be wise, they become fools.**

**Mr. Big Stuff**- Can't you just hear Jean Knight singing "Who do you think you are?" The greatest sales manual of all time says we're not supposed to play favorites. Sinner of the huge proportion that I am, I repent once again. When your livelihood (ministry, I aspire) is only open 4 hours a day, do you have at least 3 of those hours disposable to be held captive by Mr. Big Stuff blowin' about himself? Further confirming that not everyone is our customer. We have to focus on our studs, not our duds. More irony, Mr. Big Stuff isn't the stud he thinks he is. With that said, I can think of multiple individuals (from both genders) fitting this personality, that keep coming back to Express Lunch with big smiles, and I really wanna think their ship has started steering towards the land of humility. Do they feel that indescribable something (Holy Spirit) that they just can't define, or put their finger on? I hope! I pray! May we be doing our job! It has to be a covert mission. We can't hit people over the head with a 40 pound Bible, or wave "the fish." We sure can't put the word "church" on the side of the building, or no one would ever come in.

**Suzy Servant**- This is your customer. This is your stud. So many times, this personality will say she came in today because she was in such a hurry looking after her kids and getting them off to school, she forgot her own lunch. This is your "to go" customer, because she only gets 30 minutes at the most for lunch. Her tab is $8-$10, when she's lucky to be making $10-$12 an hour in Crossville, TN. She's always happy, grateful and hopeful. She knows this world doesn't owe her anything, and that her debt has been paid, and by whom. What she has, Mr. Big Stuff can't buy. I wasn't kidding when I said we have the best customers. Suzy Servant is our spokesmodel. She comprises the greatest percentage of who we get the privilege of serving every day. Yes, it kinda feels like a cliché, but the meek shall inherit the earth.

**The Shopper**- This is the person who would drive all over town to see who had the lowest gas price, so they could save a few pennies. Saving pennies costs dollars. I'll spend a nickel to make a buck, but not spend a dollar to save a nickel. If price is all that matters, this is not your customer. The shopper wants something for free, if he or she can get it. "Free" can oftentimes end up being expensive, and I personally don't want any part of it. At first, I couldn't believe how Express

Lunch customers would not ask how much something costs. Folks come into Express Lunch because they want fresh, fast, friendly, and hopefully fun. We have to put the **F** into fun!

**The Chef**- In the early days of Express Lunch, we had an individual in the kitchen who loved being called the chef. Of course, I facetiously started this title, and "the chef" was so proud of it, the name stuck. Ever known a person built really large physically that people called "Tiny?" We're pretty much talking about the same thing here. The chef never attended a day of culinary school, but always wanted to add "scud" missiles to our menu that no one could pronounce, or wanted to purchase. My favorite of the numerous chef stories I could tell, but don't, is when I turned in an order for a peanut butter sandwich. I had a mom out front with an inconsolable child. What else do you offer to attempt to hit the mark for an inconsolable child?

When I turn in the order that reads "peanut butter sandwich" verbatim, I'm immediately barraged with the interrogation. "Don't they want jelly?" "No" (answered in Myron Monotone's mundane voice). "What kind of jelly do they want?" "They don't want jelly. " "What kind of bread do they want?" "Wheat" (we put everything on wheat, unless otherwise specified). "Do they want it toasted?" "No." By now, cheffy poo is so totally perplexed and exasperated, he says, "They just want peanut butter and bread?" My final response started out so proper with my attempted Miss Congeniality meets Fairy Godmother voice replying, "just bread and peanut butter, because (which now gave way to my Chris Farley/Matt Foley voice, saying) IT'S A PEANUT BUTTER SANDWICH!" Why do we think we have to turn everything into rocket science? Why can't we simply listen with the ears that God gave us to listen with, and read with the eyes that God gave us to read with? It's the same with the sacrifice that was made for us for our salvation. Only one took the nails for all; only one ever defeated death. It's that simple.

Thank you Lord for allowing me to let You be You, and take over running Express Lunch for us! Why do we make a big deal out of little things, when the only thing that matters is judgement day? **James 4:6: But he giveth more grace. Wherefore he saith God resisteth the proud, but giveth grace unto the humble.**

**Polecat**- Be careful of the polecat, cuz when they say "to tell you the truth," they ain't tellin' the truth. There's often a real bad residual stink that comes from dealin' with a polecat, too. **Proverbs 19:9: A false witness shall not be unpunished, and he that speaketh lies shall perish.**

**Foghorn Leghorn**-This is the guy who starts stuttering like Foghorn Leghorn, when he senses that you've caught on to the fact that he's not been telling you the truth, and is full of it. When he starts saying (in Foghorn Leghorn voice) "w w well I, I, I, s s say b b boy," you officially know what you're dealin' with. I dealt with this very same scenario with a power washing operation recently. These cats dance around like a cat on a hot stove, once they know you're on to 'em.

**Slick Willy**- There was a time when I first got to take a look at a fella that was supposed to be running for president. My immediate initial impression was "I've seen that sly grin before on every used car lot in Nashville." Well, we ended up electing this individual twice. How's that for accountability? Remember when Mitch Ryder did the song "Devil In A Blue Dress?" Slick Willy had a fondness for blue dresses, which he lied and denied about. The Lord can warn us, and remind us in all kinds of ways and songs. How many times have dresses of all kinds of colors been man's Achilles' heel? Man's textbook says we decide within 10 seconds whether we like someone or not, and I have to agree to some degree. I sure wouldn't wanna say I don't like Slick Willy; I just never wanted to buy what he was sellin'. Everything is sales, huh? I decided years ago that I was gonna love everybody, because if I didn't, I was the one who was missing out. I tried once to remind my buddy Eeyore that the greatest sales manual of all time tells us that we're supposed to love everybody. He slowly replied "it doesn't mean we've gotta like em."

**Proverbs 19:1: "Better is the poor that walketh in his integrity, than he that is perverse in his lips, and is a fool."**

<u>Lady Hillary</u>- My initial impression of Slick Willy's spouse reminded me of how Shakespeare's Lady MacBeth wanted to be king more than her husband MacBeth did. I don't nail 'em all at first sight, but these two were really easy to read. Not only do we have to be wary of those with agendas and schemes, we most importantly have to make sure we're not the ones with the agendas and schemes.

<u>The Lollipop Licker</u>- This might be the most important and dangerous personality to study. You know how an Eskimo kills a wolf? The Eskimo will take a very sharp knife and coat it repeatedly with animal blood until it freezes into many layers of a blood lollipop. The knife is then placed butt end into the ground until the wolf comes along. The wolf loves the taste of that blood all the way down to the sharp blade, where the wolf then goes crazy with all of the blood he's getting to lap up now. The only problem is, that wolf is ultimately and fatally consumed in his own blood that he thinks he can't get enough of. Very similar to those of us who think we wanna be king or queen of something. Ever had to work with a lollipop licker? Somebody who gets a lil taste of man's success in "this world?" They get consumed with greed, and keep wanting more, and more,

and more, and more. There's never enough of what these folks think they're chasing. Ultimately, whatever the lollipop licker was obsessing over the whole time is what causes their final demise. The greatest sales manual of all time warns that we're not to be consumed by our own lusts. It's very important that we never become a lollipop licker.

**Lil Darth**- Worked with a lil feller who wanted to "take over the whole universe" of this particular company. Lil Darth had decided within the first 10 seconds that he wasn't gonna like me. I guess it mighta had something to do with me being about the first person this bunch ever hired with a few credentials, and who wasn't a cousin, to a cousin, to a cousin, to a cousin of a current employee. I was just trying to feed my family to the best of my ability (theme sure keeps popping up). Lil Darth tried every way he could to get me fired, but in the meantime, always had innocent prey in his sights, and on his radar. Outside our main office was a meeting room which I referred to as the "gas chamber." This was where Lil Darth would gather his immediate subordinates, who were often used as pawns, which we'll refer to as "Hitler's youth." After all of these characters had settled into the gas chamber, an innocent servant would lastly be brought in to be "corrected," written up, or was just the latest chosen one that the wanna be regime thought they had to tell themselves they were gonna have a problem with.

I'll never forget the time Lil Darth called me into the gas chamber to get me to incriminate a co-worker who was known to only confide in me. Lil Darth starts out with "Mike, I was wrong about you, and wanna bury the hatchet." Well of course, I came back with my "Gomer" persona and said, "Why would you have a hatchet to bury with me?" I continued with innocent naiveté until the interrogation was over, and was eventually granted permission to exit the gas chamber. Would this be a good example of a lollipop licker? Why do we seek our own finite power and glory, when we could pursue the power and glory of God? There's always something we can learn from everybody. What TO DO, and also what NOT to do.

**1 Corinthians 9:19: "For though I be free from all men, yet have I made myself servant unto all, that I might gain the more."**

We've spent a lot of time talking about workplace characters. It's because we spend a great deal of time in the workplace. We spend more time with co-workers who we did not choose to be with, versus the time we get to spend with those we choose to be with outside of work. Many of us have been previously and currently oppressed in the workplace. If you're currently in this position, I don't want you to feel alone. At the time, workplace oppression feels like it's gonna last forever. Please remember, there's only One Forever. When you eventually overcome it, a much greater person has been built. Please hang in there **peculiar treasure**, and continually keep your eyes on the Prize. **Ecclesiastes 9:17: "The words of wise men are heard in quiet more than the cry of him that ruleth among fools."**

> **Matthew 5:44: "But I say unto you, Love your enemies, bless them that curse you, do good to them that hate you, and pray for them which despitefully use you, and persecute you."**

<u>**Young Bull**</u>- He's the one on top of the hill overlooking the valley full of beautiful cows, and is all excited. He says to the Old Bull "Hey, let's run down there and make friends with a couple of them cows." Picture the Warner Brothers cartoon "Which way did he go, George?" on that last quote.

<u>**Old Bull**</u>- He's the one who slowly says (Sam Elliott voice) to the young bull, "What do ya say we walk down there and make friends with "ALL OF THE COWS?" This is a very good example of how we can't get overzealous, and we have to take our time "to think before we do," which is a behavior we need to learn more and more as we hopefully mature. I can't tell you how many times in my younger days that I jumped head first into swimming pools that didn't have any

water, without ever even looking first to see if there was any water in those pools. The consequences can be very painful. I've had to learn so many times over the years, we simply have to slow down, to get more accomplished over the long run.

**The Teenager**- Where do I begin? First of all, "IT'S NOT THEIR FAULT!" Picture Chris Farley doing his Matt Foley character saying that last quote. The teenager these days might not be the most socially versed. IT'S NOT THEIR FAULT! Their whole life, all they've ever done is play "texty texty" and "kideo games." How should they be expected to know how to talk to someone? How should they be expected to have a work ethic? Have you ever seen a teenager after a long hard day sittin' in school, go straight to their bedroom to lie around for a full evening of kideo games and TV? That's a talent I had as a pre-teen, but fortunately grew out of. If you don't have bill deadlines pending, where's the urgency for initiative?

Ever go into those fast food joints? There's always at least one teenager standing around with that homogenous pose. You know, the one Adam and Eve had when they first found out they didn't have anything on, and were trying to cover themselves? The teenager is covering up down there, because they're afraid they're about to wet their britches, because they might actually have to talk to somebody. I can't tell ya how many times we've been blessed and covered up with all kinds of customers and then the phone rings. The teenager looks around in utter terror to see if anybody is gonna get the phone. In the heat of battle, I then have to say to the teenager, "Answer the phone." The teenager says, "What do I say?" I then look the teenager directly in the eyes and say in my best Miss Congeniality/Fairy Godmother voice:

"SAY H E L L O." Remember in the old days, when there were landlines, and we all raced our siblings to see who could answer the phone the fastest? We also had to go through the mom or the dad to get to talk to a girl. Now they just hookup anytime they want on their own personal phone that somehow gets magically paid for them each month. We probably don't want to know what other easily accessible elements are lurking through their phones. Why should we expect the teenager at the counter of these fast food joints to aggressively take initiative and understand urgency, when food just magically shows up in the fridge at home? How about the teenager whose parent(s) have different priorities, and there's nothing in the fridge at home? We have to pray very hard for our teenagers. I would love for a bazillion teenagers to be reading this right now, because there's tremendous OPPORTUNITY out there, and there's ALWAYS A POSITIVE to every scenario. Get up and move, you **peculiar treasures**. I want you to be a success! Most importantly, I want you to be a True Success.

When a mom tells a teenager she made their sandwich for school lunch, and the teenager says "ok," they don't get it. How can there be any other answer other than THANK YOU?! All the way from my mom to my grandma, to my wife, to my daily walk brother Tommy's killer homemade pizza buffets, I have to say "thank you" multiple times during the course of a meal. Can't help it, I love to eat, and I'm very grateful. Is there any other option than to say thank you? When I was a kid, my dad told me that this world never owed us nothin. Because it came from my dad, I listened, and funny thing, he was right. My dad and I had a 2 step process. He told me what to do, and I did it! Talking back was not an option. **Exodus 20:12 "Honour thy father and thy mother: that thy days may be long upon the land which the Lord thy God giveth thee."** I never knew what the word entitlement was supposed to mean until almost 30 years after I was a teenager. I guess I was always too busy working all of those years to have ever heard the term. We never heard that word growing up. Who came up with the word entitlement? Thanks to our Savior's sacrifice, we're all entitled to His Eternal Kingdom, if we simply surrender. Thank you Lord!

We currently have a homeschooled teenager on staff that is doing a really good job, and I'm very proud of her. When a teenager comes into Express Lunch for a job and says "thank you" for anything, I'm very hopeful that we have someone we can work with. There's nothing better than when a teenager comes in displaying evidence that their parents have "shown them the way in which to go." That's being THE EXCEPTION. That's OPPORTUNITY! In all seriousness, I have great empathy for the teenager. We weren't affluent, but my sister and I were very blessed to have 2 sets of really good parents residing next to each other on the farm. Nowadays, a kid is lucky if they have one good parent. **Psalm 27:10: When my father and my mother forsake me, then the Lord will take me up.**

**The Critic**- Which I sure pray I don't ever come across as. The critic is the one who's always trying to find a speck in someone else's eye, when there's a redwood in their own. For our learning purposes, I have given actual facts from what different personalities and characters have done. My intent is not to be belittling or demeaning to anyone, but to provide examples for our learning purposes. This is why I don't use real names in our examples. When illustrating characters, I very frequently use the words "we" and "us" to accept accountability for how "we" do things, even if it is the discussion of a practice I don't adhere to. I don't wanna hurt anybody, I want to help everybody. Since I personally require the facts, I have to report the facts. I report, you decide. **Psalm 19:14: "Let the words of my mouth, and the meditation of my heart, be acceptable in thy sight, O Lord, my strength, and my redeemer."** For all of our critics and scorekeepers out there, please keep track that there are more examples of me not doing what I should have done, than stories about anyone else's shortcomings. If you don't believe it, wait 'til we get to the "Real McCoy." When we stand up, stand up for Jesus as I'm aspiring to do by journaling this journey, we must be prepared to be a visible target on satan's radar. If we're living a sinful life, why would satan come after us when he already owns us? **Galatians 1:10: "For do I now persuade men, or God? Or do I seek to please men? for if I yet pleased men, I should not be the servant of Christ."**

**The Court Jester**- My first year in college, I was in the music department at Butler University in Indianapolis, Indiana. I almost always stayed late in the practice rooms, and worked real hard. One night I came back to my room, and my roommate, his girlfriend, and a football player she was tutoring by the name of "Murph" was in the room. Murph was well known to everyone on campus as the meanest there was. It wasn't uncommon to watch Murph turn a guy upside down in a trash can, and walk away laughing. Upon my arrival back to the room this particular evening, I see Murph sitting at my desk, so I very stoically and nonchalantly say (actually in my own voice-maybe a lil Bob Newhart?) "you're in my chair," and keep looking at the guy. While Murph kept looking at me as well, trying to cypher the whole thing out (there's a reason he was there for tutoring), my roommate, thinking I'm gonna get killed, is saying to me "Do you know who you're talking to?" It only took a few seconds later, and even Murph figured it out. He starts laughing, saying to the other two "I like this guy!" I learned right then – the good thing about me is nobody ever takes me seriously. You know what the bad thing is about me? Nobody ever takes me seriously. The Court Jester has all kinds of buddies, but real friends are a precious commodity. **Proverbs 18:24: "A man that hath friends must shew himself friendly: and there is a friend closer than a brother."**

**Gomer**- Probably my most frequently utilized persona. If I'm doing my Gomer persona with a "nice" person, they'll treat me kindly and with empathy. Now of course, this nice person could still be saying to themselves "bless his heart." If I'm doing my Gomer with a "not-so-nice" person, they'll be condescending, treat me like I'm stupid, and try to steamroll me. Try doing a Gomer when you're with man's stereotypical salesperson who displays they're absolutely "of this world." They really try to steamroll ya. Why do I "play" Gomer to begin with? When dealing with people, YOU'VE GOT TO KNOW WHAT YOU'VE GOT! Playing Gomer is a real good way of bringing out someone's "true colors."

On multiple occasions at Express Lunch, I've sat with people who'll say "I feel something about this place." I'll say in my Gomer voice "feel what?" I act like I don't have a clue, and this is the first time someone has ever "felt something special" at Express Lunch. They'll then say "I don't know; there's something special here." I'll then ask, "Are you a Jesus person?" Every time, they'll answer "yes." I then lean forward, look 'em in the eyes, and softly say, "It's the Holy Spirit. We surrender the place to the Lord, and He blesses us way beyond our imagination." One of my favorites is the verse mentioned earlier, **Proverbs 16:3,** which says **"Commit thy works unto the LORD, and thy thoughts shall be established."**

**The Evangelist**- This salesperson represents the greatest product of all time: Jesus Christ! At Express Lunch we provide a matching retirement fund for our employees. Why? Because such a retirement match is just about unheard of with a restaurant proprietorship. With an eternal 401K, the evangelist's Employer offers benefits no one can match.

<u>**Your Servant**</u>- Quite possibly the biggest sinner of all personalities. I've personally had to suffer through every one of this guy's mistakes. Come judgement day, Your Servant wouldn't change places with anyone, because he knows he has to be accountable for all he's done right or wrong, and he cares only about the golden opportunity of thanking the Savior face to face for all He's done. Your Servant is a very private person, but will expose himself to all of the critics if it means at least one person achieves eternal life. Your servant loves all humankind, but with no offense, wants to try his hardest to be like Christ. **1 John 2:6: "He that saith he abideth in him ought himself also so to walk, even as he walked."**

<u>**The Square Peg-**</u> We saved the best for last. **Matthew 20:16 says, "So the last shall be first, and the first last: for many be called, but few chosen."** Feel like you don't fit in with man's society? Congratulations – you've been chosen for bigger and better things! This personality has the greatest potential of becoming a **peculiar treasure** and achieving True Success. Notice how many times in our lives there's a fine line between failure and success? Ever seen square pegs who are filled with absolute vitriol for the world and our creator? I refer to these folks as a "hard sell." If you can win this personality to Christ, you've got a committed member of the Lord's Army who will serve with full conviction. The

apostle Paul always comes to mind when I think of a hard sell. If this personality describes you, and you're sick and tired of being sick and tired all of the time, the ultimate relief awaits. Let go, and let God.

Ever been picked on, bullied, or called names for being different? I can only recall being called weird two times. Each time, I immediately said thank you for the compliment, because I don't want anything to do with being part of a homogenous herd. Ever been called a misfit? Ever felt like a misfit? Good for you – congratulations! With a bowed head and folded hands, the ultimate opportunity awaits. It can be a sad, lonely, and frustrating existence until a square peg figures out the Only thing that matters in this world. When this happens, the reward is indescribable. **Matthew 5:5: "Blessed are the meek: for they shall inherit the earth."**

Why have we taken all of this time to study so many additional personalities we could potentially encounter? First and foremost, each one of these personalities are inside of every one of us to some degree, and have to be identified. Always putting ourselves under self examination, to identify our own strengths and weaknesses. **Lamentations 3:40: "Let us search and try our ways, and turn again to the Lord."** The personalities that portray a more positive nature we need to nurture, cultivate, and promote within ourselves. Ultimately our good traits can become great traits. We're all sinners. We have to beware of the not-so-positive traits inside all of us that can rear their ugly heads (or ugly rears) at any time, and NEVER FULLY BECOME ONE OF THESE PERSONALITIES! After using these personalities for our own self examination, we can then access these personalities at any time to determine who we are dealing with. We now know how to approach these types of people, and how to effectively communicate with them. **Romans 3:23 "For all have sinned and fall short of the glory of God."**

I can't tell you how many times I would LISTEN to "driver" personalities blow about themselves, while I would sit there and determine what personality type was in front of me. With each word, they're telling me how to "sell them." Then I might go even further, if necessary, and break the individual down into one of these few of my own names that I've just shared with you. I can tell you I'm a servant, but to this day I can't tell you which one of man's 4 personality types I'm personally supposed to be. I hope I can draw from any of these 4 personalities at any time. I once had a co-worker cock their head and say to me, "I can't figure you out." My response was "Perfect, I've got you right where I want you." I hope I'm perceived as a **peculiar treasure**! Through proper "wax on, wax off," as Mr. Miyagi from "Karate Kid" would say, I believe we all can buff (rebuke) and polish (admonish) ourselves into becoming proficient at acquiring positive traits from all of these 4 basic personalities.

Since THERE'S ALWAYS A POSITIVE, let's take the

positives from each of man's 4 personalities, and see how we can build a better servant:

**The Driver**- Drivers are a very strong personality (servants can't be weak at anything). Typically they have a go-get-it-done or whatever-it-takes personality (we sure don't wanna be lukewarm at anything).

**Expressive**- Very outgoing and enthusiastic, with a high energy level (enthusiasm sells). They enjoy helping others, and are particularly fond of socializing (EVANGELISM BABY!).

**Analytical**- Very deep and thoughtful. They're serious and purposeful individuals (what greater purpose than to serve our Lord?). They set very high standards, so they have very high standards of performance personally and professionally (we'd better set very high standards, and lead by our example).

**Amiable**- Very patient and well-balanced individual (when witnessing, if we aren't well balanced, we might run people off from the Lord forever). They're quiet and witty (the less we say, the more it means). They're sympathetic, kind, and inoffensive (refer to miss congeniality whenever "wax on" "wax off" needs applying). An amiable is easy going and everybody likes the amiables (wow, any better than the amiable to be out in the trenches for our Lord?).

There's no way we can limit God's creation into just 4 personalities. It's not a one size fits all. Consider the small sampling of personalities I've personally encountered and experienced that I just shared with you. There's no imagining the infinite amount of personalities our God can create. I hate to break it to some folks, but mother nature didn't lean to one side to break wind, and poof, we all just showed up.

## • • • •
# THE SIGNS

When I was 36, my sales position had me calling on a lot of stores such as Walmart. At the Walmart in Crossville, I made such great friends with a man whose actual name is Steve Lamb, that his peers would call us "blood brothers." One day Steve asked me if I was "saved." I said "I sure hope so, cuz I love the Lord more than anything." Next thing I know, Steve has me in a back office praying for me. Sinner that I am, I couldn't help but sneak a peek to make sure a grown man was actually weeping and praying for my soul. For the next 7-10 days, I felt like I was floating through air and untouchable. Since then, I've always joked that I was "saved by a Lamb." How's that for a sign? Of course, we all know the real Lamb of God who was brought to save us all from permanent death. I'm sure I'm not the smartest. The Almighty made sure Steve Lamb was placed in my path to properly send me in the right direction, and I can never thank the Source or the vessel enough. **John 1:29: "The next day John seeth Jesus coming unto him, and saith,**

Behold the Lamb of God, which taketh away the sin of the world."

You know how when a lot of folks turn 40, they have what man calls a "mid-life crisis?" When I was 40, I had a mid-life "Christis," I was waking up with songs that I had never heard before. Funny thing, these songs that also no one else had ever heard before were faith songs, which reminded me who the real love of my life was. I wasn't a pianist or guitarist who was intentionally sitting down to write secular pop songs for $. I was the last person in this world who wanted anything to do with "music row" or the music business. I didn't know why I was receiving these songs, or what to do with them. I did know Who the songs came from, and the importance of doing something to display obedience and gratitude.

In a little over a year's time, I documented 52 songs. I had a duty to the author. Six of these songs were performed in churches, which provided no greater privilege or thrill, to think something like that could come through a simple servant like me. After a whole lot of lost sleep caused by these middle-of- the-night direct dialogues, I eventually figured out that these songs were brought for me to journal my journey. My job is to help others know how He'll talk to us, if we'll just listen. How He wants to use us, if we'll simply let Him. I was on that indescribable ride of transformation, and finally had to say Lord, I get it. I'm very tired. Can I please stop documenting, so I can work for you in other ways? This last week, I woke up with a song I had never heard before, and sang it to my wife. She said, "I've never heard that before." I said, "Exactly, me neither." I would encourage everyone to journal their own unique journey, just as I'm continuing to do with you now. This experience has taught me a ton. Most importantly, I've learned how Your Servant is the personality that needs the most improvement.

Remember when I told ya the greatest group I was ever a part of was Wayne Shadden's Thursday night men's Bible study? I attended this group at a time when I was probably most broken. A servant I had only known through this group that we'll call "The Real McCoy" had everyone gather around me one night, while he led the men in prayer for ME!

After my tour of duty with the Wayne Shadden group. I hadn't seen The Real McCoy for probably 7 or 8 years, until the Friday afternoon before Good Friday, April 3rd, 2020. I was walking in the parking lot of our local Rural King, and I kept looking at a fella walking out that I thought looked like The Real McCoy. I kept staring, and thought that can't be him. The Real McCoy was not only a lot bigger in girth, I even thought he was 3 or 4 inches taller than what I was seeing. I kept thinking if this is my old friend, he'll eventually look over at me so I can say hey, and thank him again for how

I'll never forget the time he stood up for me. This man that I couldn't take my eyes off of had a hollowed out trance of a stare, and a scowl on his face that clearly said I wanna be left alone. I did exactly what his face told me to do, without ever looking towards me, or saying a word. I have a saying, "If in doubt, stay out," so I did.

Sunday Morning, April 5th, 2020. We're running through the songs at the church I play drums at every Sunday Morning. I see where a brother from the Wayne Shadden group had tried to call me. Thinking something must be wrong, I hurried to call him back right before church started. My friend told me The Real McCoy had taken his life the day before.

What are the odds of not seeing someone for 7-8 years, and then "all of a sudden" you see this fellow servant the very afternoon before he takes his own life?

God is always laying signs and opportunities to serve Him in our path and in our lap. There are no "coincidences" in this world. Our God continually defies all the odds. We have to LISTEN, and take heed to His instructions. Yes, the most important thing we'll ever do yesterday, today, or tomorrow is LISTEN.

A couple of days later, I sent a text to Wayne Shadden around suppertime, asking him to call me at his convenience. Wayne called me immediately. That's how he is, always cocked and ready to serve. Knowing that Wayne and The

Real McCoy had been the best of friends for years, I told Wayne I was calling to repent. Wayne told me that our friend had just been to see him the day before he had walked right past me in that parking lot. He shared that our friend had lost a lot of weight, and that he himself did everything he could to try to bring our friend back in. Wayne assured me that there was nothing I could have done to change the outcome.

The facts are the facts. The fact is, when I needed The Real McCoy, he was there for me. When he needed me, I didn't do a thing. Clear and simple, cut and dried. Unlike the folks who think they wanna tell themselves something that never happened over and over until they actually believe something that never happened, I have to have the facts. I have to have the truth, and I have to live for the Truth. This is why I aspire to live for the Lord, because there's only one Truth. The fact is I didn't give Mr. McCoy that full 100% no more, no less, effort. I didn't give him anything, and I have to be accountable. "What if?" What if I'd said "Hey Mr. McCoy, is that you? What if I had "sold" my friend into stickin' around this place? What if I'd done my job, and checked on him?

In Luke 9:62, the Lord says we have to keep our hands to the plow, because if we look back, we aren't fit for the kingdom of heaven. The last thing I can do is forever beat myself up, or satan wins, and one victory is more than he ever deserved. I feel like a lot of the different personality characters I've encountered and shared with you are portrayed in a negative nature. Satan is a very bad dude, and will plant as many skaliwags, rascals, and just plain ding dangin' doozies in our path as possible. We're the ones who have to identify who they are, and be cocked and ready whenever we encounter them.

# • • • •
# PERSPECTIVE

Another question I've always loved asking people over the years is "if you had just one wish in this whole wide world, what would it be?" The vast majority have responded "No more cancer," or "No more Alzheimer's." My mom had breast cancer, and her mom was eventually freed from the debilitation of Alzheimer's disease. I'll never forget one guy saying he "would wish for a million more wishes," which might be my all-time favorite response. My answer has always been "I would wish for Eternity for all." Through our Lord's sacrifice, we all have been given the opportunity for salvation. Eternal life is the only thing that isn't temporary. As despicable as cancer is, it is still temporary. As lamentable as Alzheimer's is, it is still temporary. Merely going with the odds, a very large portion of that fella's million wishes is probably gonna have something to do with the temporary pleasures that are involved in this world. As good as every milkshake I ever encountered was, none of 'em lasted for long. They all disappeared real fast. Scientists say that the temperature of the earth's core is between 9,000 and 11,000 degrees Fahrenheit. Seeing that man is the one doing the measuring, they might be off a little bit, but it's still way too hot for me. There's not enough sunscreen in this world to help anybody whose final destination is the opposite of heaven. I would not wish the opposite of Eternity upon anyone! **Timothy 2:4: "God wants all men to be saved and to come to a knowledge of the truth."**

# TRUE SUCCESS AND THE FINAL VICTORY

Growing up, all of our dads were the same age as Bobby Knight, the Indiana Basketball coach who was called "The General." When you're raised on a farm in Indiana, guess who all our dads thought they wanted to be like? Knight was a hard disciplinarian (driver). You should research him and formulate your own opinion. It felt like my peers and I were the last of a disciplined era where we had to have a work ethic. For the first 30 years of my life, my dad was mean, mad, and my biggest critic. I cannot, and will not repeat the things that were said to me. I finally stood up to him one day, and told him no more. For the last 24 years, guess who my biggest fan and cheerleader was? He BELIEVED in me.

Over a year ago, my dad spent his final round-up in bed for 7 weeks and 3 days. Every other weekend, I would make the 901 mile round trip back to the farm to be with him. The last trip we made, I arrived in a dark bedroom with my sister at his side. I looked down, and asked myself which was bigger – my dad or a set of bagpipes? His hands were folded, and what he slowly said, we'll never forget. "Heavenly Father, please make room for me, and please take good care of my family." My sister and I then cocked our heads and peripherally looked at each other as if to think, "Did we just hear what we thought we just heard come out of our dad's mouth?" In unison and with total astonishment, my sister and I said "Amen." Our dad then said "Amen." He did it! Before it was too late, he did it! Nine days later, our dad took his last breath on earth. In years past, I cannot tell you how many times I had to hear my dad use God's name improperly. I can tell you how many times I had ever heard him pray before: NEVER!

My dad always said, "Son, ain't none of us gonna make it outta here alive." The good thing about my dad was, he was always right. The bad thing about my dad was, he was always right. My dad was right again; his body didn't make it outta here alive. His soul did! My dad wanted his ashes buried on the farm. When it came time to eulogize him, my prayer was, "Lord, may I not shed a tear, so I don't shame and dishonor my dad with a cry baby." I retold my dad's only audible prayer I had ever heard in front of his closest family and friends, as I prayed for their souls as well. Flanked by my wife and daughter who were soaking my shoulder on both sides with tears, I did not shed a tear myself. My dad was the greatest dad in the whole wide world. You know why? He was MINE. If we can love our dad as much as I do mine, how much should or can we love our Father? **Romans 10:13: For whosoever shall call upon the name of the Lord shall be saved.**

**TRUE SUCCESS** is loving the Lord more than anything, and wanting to serve our Lord with everything. In the end, my dad loved the Lord more than anything. My dad did his job the best he knew how, and to the best of his ability. He was the greatest provider, and very generous to us. His way of serving the Lord was by serving his family and everyone around him. Look up all of the celebrities and billionaires who call themselves Atheists, or say they don't believe in God. How can someone believe with full conviction in NOTHING?! Sorry to not pattycake it to ya, but when all of these celebrities and billionaires don't make it outta here alive, their temporary thrill is done. They're nothing more than dust; game over. He who doesn't believe in Jesus shall perish and not receive eternal life.

I can flat out point blank tell you right now what this journal is about. It's about preparing ourselves with the proper tools necessary to prepare others for the Kingdom of Heaven. True success has been laid in your lap. Doctors can save lives, but you can save souls! Life is a very precious temporary thing; an Eternal soul is everything. You have the tools. You know that everything is sales, and you know how to sell. How do you sell? By being REAL! Just like the drum students, do you sell with your brain, or your heart? You sell from the heart! A heart that was given to you by the almighty creator God Almighty! We had to go through all of the customer service examples to learn that there is something greater: Customer Servitude! Through Customer Servitude, we utilize "greater is He that's in us." Since we love the Lord more than anything, we can now apply customer servitude to serving humankind with everything. Now when we go to do our job in the great commission, we have these parallels to draw from:

Sales = EVANGELISM

Customer Servitude = Serving the Lord by loving and serving humankind the same way we do our Lord.

You're ready, **peculiar treasures**. Go tell it on the mountain! Go sell everyone you know! Go serve everyone you see! We have to bring in everyone we can, so no one misses out on the Kingdom of Heaven. **Matthew 28:19-20: "Go ye therefore, and teach all nations, baptizing them in the name of the Father, and of the Son, and of the Holy Ghost: Teaching them to observe all things whatsoever I have commanded you: and, lo, I am with you always, even unto the end of the world. Amen."**

Thank you for sharing this journey with me. The stories weren't hard to tell. If you've lived it, you don't have to make anything up. I hope I have helped you in at least one way, shape, or form. If you aren't living for the Lord, I beg you now with all that I've got, before it's too late, to live your life for the One who lived His life for you. Simply through a little humility and obedience, I've gotten to live an abundantly Blessed life. If I can ever serve you in any way, I'm really easy to find at Express Lunch in Crossville, Tennessee. If you ever get to Express Lunch, please take a really good look around. Almost all the items on the walls are gifts given from customers. I've been amazed how many people have never been in before, and still come in bearing gifts their first time! People just have it in their hearts, and bring gifts. Every now and then I'll have real strong folks of the faith say to me, "I just don't know what's happening to this world." Don't let anybody fool ya; there are a lot of really good people in this world, and I get the privilege of witnessing every day. Call me, text me, email me, because there's no greater honor than to serve. If you have a group you want me to speak with, please use me. In the meantime, keep your hands to the plow, and never look back.

Printed in the United States
By Bookmasters